A
Formal
Introduction to
Critical Thinking

Third Edition

By
Dr. Daniel Kern

978-1-329-86773-4
Copyright 2016
Daniel R. Kern

Table of Contents

Preface

This text, as the title suggests, is a formal introduction to critical thinking. There are a number of approaches to teaching Critical Thinking. Most of them tend toward informal approaches, in which students spend a lot of time reading newspaper articles and watching video clips and are instructed to evaluate the argumentation in them. I believe that this is the wrong approach to teaching Critical Thinking. The analogy I use to explain my approach to my students is that this is like sending soldiers to war without ever having gone through basic training. I ask my students what the result of this might be, and they are quick to respond that these soldiers would likely die very quickly, because they don't know what they are doing. In order to succeed on the battlefield, a person needs physical training and education in the ways of war. I believe that formal logic is to a person's mind or reason what basic training is to a person's body. It is training in and the strengthening of the mental "muscles" that one needs to be a successful reasoner.

I use war as an analogy not by accident. I believe that the rational stakes in our world are high, and that people are involved in an intense battle for their beliefs. There are a number of people who would be happy to overcome us rationally and control and dominate us by convincing us to believe what they want us to believe, whether it is true or false. The primary enemies in this battle are advertisers, politicians, and religious leaders. This is not to say that there is anything wrong with politics or religion (I will have nothing positive to say about advertising); just that these are the primary areas in our lives in which people try to convince us to believe what they want us to believe, and in which people often resort to bad arguments to convince us. The only adequate preparation for withstanding these attempts to control us is to have a rigorous training in the fundamental concepts of logic and reason, which is Deductive or Formal Logic. Hence this text, of which about 80% deals with deductive logic. With good basic training in the rules of rational engagement, I believe students will be more successful students of life.

At the same time, since this text is designed for a one-semester Critical Thinking course, I have simplified the formal instruction somewhat. In Categorical Logic, I have used only Venn Diagrams, since they are faster and more efficient tools for analyzing arguments than the complex rules of mood, figure, distribution, etc. In Sentential Logic, I have limited the operators to the Negation, Conjunction, Disjunction, and Conditional, since the Biconditional can be formed from these and is an uncommon operator. In Natural Deduction, I have pared the set of derivation rules down to a small set, which seems to me sufficient to do the most common derivations.

Preface

In the end, I hope to have fashioned a worthwhile introduction to Critical Thinking, which avoids the excesses of informality and lack of rigor on the one end and of overly difficult technical logic on the other.

vocab
logic
reason
arguments
rhetorical
situation

Chapter 1: Introductory Concepts

1.1 – Critical Thinking, Logic and Arguments

"Critical Thinking," as we will use it in this course, is a branch of the philosophical discipline of *Logic*. **Logic is the study of argument**. Another way of saying this is that logic is the study of human *reasoning*. The characteristic that is most often associated with how humans differ from other animals is that humans reason, while other animals don't. [1] **Reason is the capacity to make decisions or come to conclusions based on the evaluation of evidence, or based on argument**. So logic is a very important study; it is the study of what makes us distinctive creatures in the world.

Arguments

When defining terms, it is not very helpful to define a term with other terms that are themselves not well defined. This is the case with defining "logic" as the study of "argument." So it will help to provide a definition of "argument." Informally, when we think of an argument, we think of a group of people, who disagree about something, voicing their opinions about what they think is the right or wrong way of viewing the issue. In addition to just voicing their opinions however, people in an argument are usually trying to *convince* the other people that their opinion is the correct one. The attempt to persuade or convince is the essential feature of arguments. To begin, we can define an argument informally as **a rhetorical situation in which someone is trying to persuade or convince someone else that his or her opinion is right or wrong**. "Rhetorical situation" refers to any situation involving communication. We can define "argument" more specifically, based on this informal definition. The *formal* definition of "argument" (the ones used by logicians) is, **a set of statements that contain at least one *premise*, one *conclusion*, and an *inference***. This definition is VERY important. It will guide everything we study in this book.

Statements

We now, though, have another definition that includes some undefined terms (statement, premise, conclusion, inference), so we should

---

[1] There may be other beings that have reason. Classically, angels and God have reason. It is also possible that there are other beings in the universe that have reason. Many contemporary biologists claim that some animals have reason (i.e., dolphins, higher-order primates, etc.). Among the beings that we know for sure exist, however, humans are the only beings that reason in the way or at the level that humans do.

define those terms as well. There are several definitions for "statement." The two simplest ones are **a sentence that is either true or false**" and "**a sentence that says something about the world**. For instance, the sentence, "The sky is blue" is a statement. It says something about the world, about the color of the sky, and it is either true or false (in this case it is true). Statements may be more complex than this one. For instance, "The governor of California asked the state government to pass a resolution declaring stem cell research legitimate and establishing a fund to promote stem cell research." This sentence still says something about the world (an action of the governor's) and it is either true or false (either the governor asked the government to do this or he didn't). All statements have these two characteristics.

Not all sentences are statements; statements are a subgroup of sentences. There are 3 types of sentences that are not statements. **Questions** are sentences, but not statements. "Are you going to get out of bed?" is a proper sentence, but it doesn't say anything about the world and it is neither true nor false (the answer to the question will be "yes" or "no", but the question itself is neither true nor false). **Commands** are also sentences but not statements. "Get out of bed!" is a is a proper sentence, but it doesn't say anything about the world and it is neither true nor false. It is just a command. Finally, expressions of emotion, sometimes referred to as "expletives" are sentences but not statements. If I stub my toe and yell "Ouch!" I have expressed a sentence, a complete thought, but I have not said anything about the world and my expression is neither true nor false.

One important clarification about statements must be made. Although statements are either true or false, it is not necessary that we *know* whether a sentence is true or false to call it a statement. For instance, "There is life on other planets" is a statement, even though we don't know whether it is true or false. It is either true or false; either there is life on other planets or not; the state of our knowledge doesn't affect that fact. Similarly, "There is a large animal living in Loch Ness in Scotland" is a statement, even though we don't know whether it is true or false.

Premises and Conclusions

An argument is composed of statements. There are two types of statements in an argument that have a special relationship to each other. The *premises* of an argument are statements that give *support* or *evidence* for another statement. In an argument between people, they are the *facts* or *information* the arguer would present to try to convince the other person(s) of whatever the arguer is trying to convince them of. The ***conclusion*** of an argument is the statement that the premises give support or evidence for, the thing the arguer is trying to convince the other(s) is true. For instance, in this argument;

> *All college students are humans.*
> *Bob is a college student.*
> **Therefore, Bob is a human.**

The italicized statements, "All students are humans" and "Bob is a student," are the premises. They are taken to give support or evidence for the statement, "Bob is a human," which is the conclusion. An argument must have AT LEAST ONE premise (if no information is being presented, there can't be an attempt to convince anyone of anything!). But there is no limit to the number of premises in an argument (except an infinite number of premises). Technically, an argument can have only ONE conclusion. If some evidence leads to more than one conclusion, then either it is not enough evidence, or there is more than one argument.

Inference

The other part of an argument is called the *inference.* I will give the formal definition of inference, then explain what it meant. **An inference is a relationship between statements in which the truth of one (or more) statements affects the probability of the truth of another statement.** The statement(s) whose truth is affecting the probability is (are) the premise(s). The statement whose probability is being affected is the conclusion. In an argument, if the premises are true, then their truth affects the probability that the conclusion is true as well. In a good argument, then, the truth of the premises will establish that the conclusion is probable. In turn, a good argument will (ideally) *motivate* or *influence* the listener to believe that the conclusion is true as well. This is a deep insight into reason and human nature. This is what it means to say that humans are rational: we are naturally convinced by arguments in which the premises support the conclusion. We can't help but be persuaded by good arguments.[2]

The term "infer" is a Latin term, meaning "to carry in." This definition is helpful in understanding the sense of "infer" in arguments – the premises infer or "carry in" the conclusion. You can't let the premises in (as true) without letting the conclusion in (as true) along with them. Thus, the

---

[2] Whether humans are always persuaded by good arguments is a matter of debate. Assuming that a person understands the argument, I argue that even though people might *act* as if they are unpersuaded by a good argument (due to emotions or some other influence), they are not in reality unpersuaded, they are just acting.

premises have a certain sort of relationship to the conclusion; namely, a *support* relationship, or an *inferential* relationship.

Arguments are divided into categories depending on the type and strength of the support relationship between the premises and the conclusion. First, the premises can support the conclusion in an absolute way; that is, the truth of the premises *guarantees* the truth of the conclusion, absolutely. For instance, consider the argument already presented:

> All students are humans.
> Bob is a student
> Therefore, Bob is a human.

In this argument, IF the premises are true (which we will assume for the moment), the conclusion MUST be true; it cannot be false. So we say the support relationship here is absolute. Arguments in which the support relationship is absolute are referred to as **DEDUCTIVE** arguments.

Now consider the argument:

> Most people who drive Jaguar cars are rich.
> Bob drives a Jaguar car.
> Therefore, Bob is rich.

In this argument, even if we take the premises to be true, there is no attempt to demonstrate absolutely that Bob is rich. The attempt is only to make the reader think it is *probable* that Bob is rich (the key here is the word "most" in the first premise). There is an attempt at persuasion here, but not in an absolute sense. Arguments in which the premises only give *probabilistic* support for the conclusion (that is, they make the conclusion probably, not necessarily) are called **INDUCTIVE** arguments. Inductive arguments that make the conclusion very probable are better (more convincing) arguments, while inductive arguments that don't make the conclusion very probable are less convincing and worse arguments.

There is one more possible (but not very interesting) support relationship. That is, the premise could have nothing at all to do with the conclusion, in which case they don't really have a support relationship (that is, their truth has no effect on the probability of the truth of the conclusion. For instance,

> The sky is blue.
> Therefore, birds fly.

Although this text has the form of an argument, the premise has no support relationship with the conclusion, so this text is not properly an argument at all.

The different support relationships can be illustrated like this:

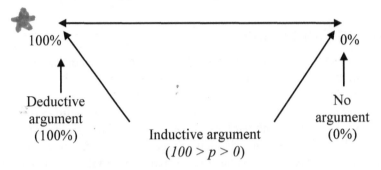

Strength of Support Relationships

Identifying Arguments

Types of arguments

Arguments, then, fall into two categories. If the premises support the conclusion absolutely (the conclusion MUST be true if the premises are true), the argument is **deductive.** If the premises give a certain amount of probability to the conclusion (greater than 0, but less than 100% probability), the argument is **inductive.** Both inductive and deductive arguments are of interest to logicians, for different reasons. Deductive arguments are interesting because of the strength of the support relationship: the premises either prove the conclusion or they don't. Deductive arguments are either/or, and they show us a lot about how arguments and inferences work. We can learn a lot about what makes arguments good or bad, from studying deductive arguments. Inductive arguments, on the other hand, are much more common than deductive arguments. Most of the arguments we encounter in everyday life are inductive, not deductive. So studying inductive arguments has a more directly practical application. My approach is to spend more time on deductive arguments, because I think we learn more about how good arguments work from the formal patterns of deductive arguments.

We are already prepared to distinguish arguments from non-arguments. An argument is a text in which there is an attempt to persuade or convince someone of something. One method of identifying a passage as an argument it to ask whether the passage has a conclusion (something being argued for or supported). Once we have determined that a passage is an argument, the next task is to determine whether it is a deductive or inductive argument. This is not an easy task; for our purposes here I will tell you whether the argument is deductive or inductive.

Evaluating Arguments

Once we have identified a passage as an argument and have identified the type of argument it is, we can begin evaluating the argument. Argument evaluation is done in two steps.[1]The first step is to evaluate the *inference* (the relationship between the premises and the conclusion).[2]The second step is to evaluate the *truth* of the premises. Although the steps are the same for both inductive and deductive arguments, the results have different names, so we will consider them separately. In the first two-thirds of this course, we will be looking at deductive arguments, so we will only cover the evaluation of deductive arguments here.

Evaluating Deductive Arguments

Evaluating for Validity

The first step in argument evaluation, again, is to evaluate the inference, or support relationship. For deductive arguments, the test question is, (positively) "IF the premises are true, is it GUARANTEED that the conclusion is true as well?" or (negatively) "IF the premises are true it is POSSIBLE for the conclusion to be false?" Take the following argument:

All German Shepherds are dogs.
All dogs are mammals.
Therefore, all German Shepherds are mammals.

IF these premises are true, the truth of the conclusion is guaranteed; it is impossible for the conclusion of THIS argument to be false (because the premises prove that the conclusion is true). We say, then, that the argument is **VALID**. Now consider this argument:

All dogs are mammals.
Some mammals have hoofs.
Therefore, some dogs have hoofs.

In this case, even if the premises are true (which they are), the truth of the premises don't guarantee the truth of the conclusion (in this case, the conclusion is in fact false). The reason is that there is no guarantee that there is any overlap between the mammals that are dogs and the mammals that have hoofs (and in fact there is no such overlap). This argument then is **INVALID**. "Valid" and "invalid" describe the successfulness of the inference, based on whether the premises prove the conclusion.

Invalid arguments with true premises

One of the most common errors that people make in evaluating arguments is to confuse arguments with true premises with valid arguments. But "true premises" does not mean "valid argument." In fact, some invalid arguments can have true premises AND a true conclusion. Look at this argument:

> All dogs are mammals.
> Some mammals are meat eaters.
> Therefore, some dogs are meat eaters.

In this case, the premises and the conclusion are all true. But the argument is INVALID. It is invalid for the same reason as the previous argument was invalid. There is no guarantee that there is any overlap between the set of mammals that are meat eaters and the set of mammals that are dogs. It is important to remember that invalid arguments can have true premises AND a true conclusion. ***The test of validity concerns the inference, not the truth of any statements.***

Valid arguments with false premises

Similarly, a valid argument may have all false premises and a false conclusion:

> All houses are more than 150 feet tall.
> The Statue of Liberty is a house.
> Therefore, the Statue of Liberty is more than 150 feet tall.

This argument is valid, because ***IF the premises were true, the conclusion would be guaranteed to be true as well.*** The inference, the support relationship, is good. However, clearly the premises are not true. This leads us to the second test, the issue of the truth of the premises.

Evaluating for Soundness

The second test only applies to VALID arguments. An argument must pass *both* tests to be a good argument, so if it has failed the first test, there is no need to proceed. Since the last example was valid, we do need to proceed to the second test. The premises in this example were clearly false. We say that a valid argument with some (at least one) false premises is UNSOUND. If the argument has ALL true premises (i.e., the first argument about dogs), it is both valid and **SOUND**.

The following chart outlines the process of evaluating a deductive argument.

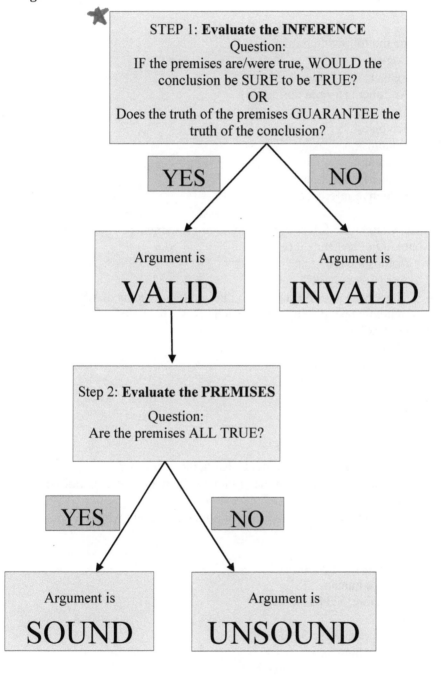

Exercises

1. Define the following terms:
    1. Logic
    2. Reason
    3. Argument (formal definition)
    4. Statement
    5. Premise
    6. Conclusion
    7. Inference
    8. Deductive inference
    9. Inductive inference

2. State whether the following sentences are statements or not. If not, say what kind of sentence it is.
    1. Robins are red. – yes
    2. Are you ready yet? – no
    3. There is an ape-like animal living in the mountains of Washington State, that people call a Sasquatch. – yes
    4. God exists. – yes
    5. I like ice cream. – yes
    6. Go to your room! no
    7. Elvis Presley is still alive. yes
    8. My team won the game! yes
    9. Yeah! no
    10. I have 13 cousins. yes

3. Evaluate the following arguments, using these criteria:
    1. Evaluate the validity of the argument. Explain why it is valid or invalid.
    2. Evaluate the soundness of the argument. Explain why it is sound or unsound.

    1. All humans have hearts.
       Sid is a human.
       Therefore, Sid has a heart.
       valid

    2. All humans have 3 heads.
       Sid is a human.
       Therefore, Sid has 3 heads.
       invalid

3. If it rains, I carry my umbrella.
   It is raining.
   Therefore, I carry my umbrella. *valid*

4. If it rains, I carry my umbrella.
   I am carrying my umbrella.
   Therefore, it is raining. *invalid*

5. No cats have horns.
   Tibby is a cat. *valid*
   Therefore, Tibby doesn't have a horn.

6. Most cats have 3 heads.
   Tibby is a cat. *invalid*
   Therefore, Tibby has 3 heads.

7. All cats are mammals.
   All mammals have lungs. *valid*
   Therefore, all cats have lungs.

8. All dogs are mammals.
   All mammals have green fur. *valid*
   Therefore, all dogs have green fur.

9. All mammals have lungs.
   Iguanas have lungs. *invalid*
   Therefore, iguanas are mammals.

10. All mammals have lungs.
    Dogs have lungs *invalid*
    Therefore, dogs are mammals

Chapter 2: Categorical Logic

• 2.1 – *Introduction*

One of the most common argument forms that humans use is the *categorical* argument. Its form is very familiar to us. Consider this valid deductive categorical argument:

> All *humans* are **mammals**.
> All ***doctors*** are *humans*.
> Therefore, all ***doctors*** are **mammals**.

Categorical arguments have several distinguishing features. First, they are composed of *categorical statements*. **A categorical statement is a statement that relates two terms.** **A term is a word or phrase that identifies a set, class or category of things** (the word "category" is the basis of the label "categorical logic").[3] A term is a *noun* or a *noun phrase*. The terms in the example above are all nouns. Any noun is a term and all terms are based on nouns. This relationship shows the closeness of logic to thought and language. When we are studying categorical arguments, we are studying the very basic structure of human thought and language. A noun, as most people remember, is a person, place, or thing. But more technically, a noun is a word that identifies a set, class, or category of things. Does this sound familiar? It's the definition of "term." So nouns, sets, categories, and terms are all referring to the same type of thing; groups of objects that we give a name to.

Terms can also be noun phrases. For instance, "the students enrolled in a critical thinking course" is a term. It represents the set of all of the students enrolled in the course. Similarly, "the planets in the universe" is a term – it represents all of the planets in the universe. Consider "the current president of the United States." This is a noun phrase, so it is a term, but it contains only one member – the current president. It's fine to have terms that have only single members.

Categorical statements are a special class of statements that have a specific form. **A categorical statement is a statement that relates (exactly) two terms.** There is a *subject term*, the subject of the sentence, and a *predicate term*, which refers to the "predicate" of the sentence (the predicate is the verb plus any modifiers or objects – more on this later). For instance, in

---

[3]   It is important to note that we often use "term" as a synonym for "word." But here, "term" is more precise – it refers to nouns and noun phrases.

All *humans* are **mammals**

"Humans" is the subject term (the subject of the sentence) and "mammals" is the predicate term.

There are two other words in the last sentence, "all" and "are." They are called, respectively, the *quantifier* and the *verb*. The verb in a categorical statement is always "is" or "are," so I won't discuss them any further. Categorical statements express how terms or sets of things are related to each other. The *quantifier* tells us how many of the first set is being related to the second set. **There are only three quantifiers in categorical logic; "All", "No" and "Some."** EVERY categorical statement must begin with one of these words (although sometimes they are understood and left out). The word "all" means that the entire first set is being included in the second set; "no" means that none of the first set is included in the second set, and "some" means, like it sounds, that some of the first set is included or not included in the second set.

Exercises

Identify the quantifier, the subject term, the verb, and the predicate term in the following categorical statements:

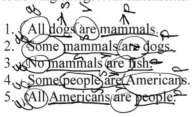

1. All dogs are mammals.
2. Some mammals are dogs.
3. No mammals are fish.
4. Some people are Americans.
5. All Americans are people.

2.2 – Diagramming Categorical Statements

A categorical argument is an argument based on relating sets of things to each other. We are going to learn a system of diagrams to evaluate categorical arguments. Let's go back to the categorical statement,

All humans are mammals.

In this statement, "all" is the quantifier, "humans" is the subject term, "are" is the verb, and "mammals" is the predicate term. The statement tells us how these two terms or sets are related to each other. (If you've ever studied set theory, categorical logic is closely related.)   What relationship is being asserted between these sets? Take a moment to try to figure it out and even to try to draw a diagram of their relationship.

The system of diagrams we're going to learn to represent these relationships is a system of circles. We will use a circle to represent each term. So, for this statement, we need a circle for "humans" and a circle for "mammals."

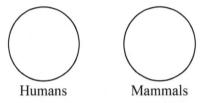

Humans   Mammals

The relationship being asserted here is that ALL the members of the set "humans" is IN the set "mammals." In other words, every human is a mammal, or nothing is a human without being a mammal (in set-theory language, humans are a *subset* of mammals). However, these circles are separated from each other, but the statement says that all of the humans are part of, or IN the set of mammals – what could we do to show that relationship? We could put the set "humans" INSIDE the set "mammals":

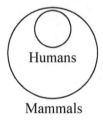

Mammals

This diagram symbolizes, or represents the relationship asserted by "all humans are mammals."

Now consider this statement: **No humans are fish**. How could we represent this relationship using circles for the terms? Well, the relationship being asserted is that NONE of the subject set, *humans*, is included in the predicate set, *s*. So our circles would just not overlap each other:

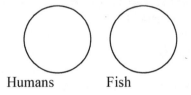

Humans   Fish

A Formal Introduction to Critical Thinking

This diagram represents or symbolizes the statement, "no humans are fish."

Next, consider this statement: **Some humans are males**. What is the statement saying about the relationship of the sets, humans and males? In logic, we take "some" to mean "at least one." So what is being asserted is that there is at least one human that is a male, but not necessarily that all humans are males. "ALL humans are mammals" had the full overlap of the human and the mammal circles; "NO humans are fish" had NO overlap between the human and the fish circle, so it seems that what is being asserted here is SOME overlap or PARTIAL overlap. This symbolization gets the main idea (although this symbolization is only partially correct):

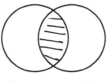

Humans   Males

The Four Categorical Statement Forms

There are a very limited number of categorical statement forms. We have already seen three of them. There is only one more. This is a very interesting fact about human reasoning and knowledge and language. It shows us how statements work: statements assert a relationship between types or classes or sets of things. They express how all or part of one set is included in or excluded from another set. Over 90% of the sentences we encounter in the world are statements. Categorical logicians claim that all of the unlimited number of statements we make can be understood in terms of only FOUR patterns.

Categorical statements each have two characteristics, called *quantity* and *quality*. The *quantity* of a statement refers to whether the statement refers to ALL of the subject set or only to SOME of the subject set. Of the statements we've seen, the ones beginning with ALL or NO (none) have this quality (it might sound strange to say a "No" statement refers to ALL of the subject class, but it does; in a moment we will see why). Statements that refer to ALL of the subject class are called *universal* statements. Statements that refer to SOME of the subject class begin with the word SOME and are called *particular* statements. These are the only two *quantities* that a categorical statement can have.

Categorical statements also have a characteristic called *quality*. The quality of the statement is either *affirmative* (think "*positive* ") or *negative*. An affirmative categorical statement expresses that all or part of the subject set is *included* in the predicate set. A negative categorical statement expresses that all or part of the subject class is *excluded* from the predicate set.

Now we have two quantities, universal and particular, and two qualities, positive and negative. All categorical statements have a quantity and a quality. Since there are two possibilities for each characteristic, we end up with 2 x 2, or four possible combinations. Here they are in a chart:

		QUANTITY	
		Universal	**Particular**
QUALITY	**Affirmative**	All humans are males (A)	Some humans are males (I)
	Negative	No humans are males (E)	Some humans are NOT males (O)

This chart shows all of the possible forms of categorical statements. The letters after each statement were assigned to them by Latin logicians to tell them apart. A handy mnemonic to help remember them is that the A and I statements are affirmative and A and I are the first two vowels of **Aff**I**r**mative. The E and O statements are negative and E and O are the first two vowels of N**E**g**O** (the Latin word for "negative"). I will now redo the chart, replacing the particular sets in the chart above with some variables. We will represent the subject term with a capital S (for subject) and the predicate term with a P (for predicate). So we get:

A Formal Introduction to Critical Thinking

		QUANTITY	
		Universal	Particular
QUALITY	Affirmative	A: All S are P	I: Some S are P
	Negative	E: No S are P	O: Some S are NOT P

Note that in this chart, the S and the P are *variables*. That means that they can stand for ANY set. For example, S or P in any categorical statement could stand for any of these sets of things; Sailors, the president of the USA, college students, smart people, elephants, galaxies, etc.

So far so good. The next step is to create circle-diagrams for each statement. We have already done this intuitively for the A, E, and I statements. But now we run into a problem. If we are going to use circle diagrams to evaluate categorical arguments, we have to have a standardized system of drawing the diagrams, or else we won't be able to figure out how the diagrams represent the argument. So now we will change everything a little to have a standard system. We will still use circles, but we will also use certain markings in the circles; shading and Xs. The particular setup we will be using is called the Venn diagram, since it was first created by John Venn in the 1880s.

Venn Diagrams for Categorical Statements

The standard form of a Venn diagram for a categorical statement is two overlapping circles – like the diagram we did for "Some humans are males." In addition to the circles, we will place two types of marking in the circles; Xs and shading. Here's what they mean:

Mark	Meaning
X in an area	There is at least one of these things.
Shading in an area	The area is EMPTY – no such things exist (in set theory, EMPTY SET)

Notice the words "in an area" associated with the markings. This expression refers to different areas on the Venn diagram, which are created by the overlap of the circles. In the following diagram, I have numbered the different areas.

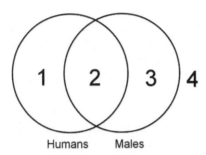

A two-circle Venn diagram has 4 areas, as shown above, each of which shows a unique relationship between the members of the two sets or classes (for our purposes, humans and males). Now we will think about the relationships being asserted in each of these areas. If anything is IN any of the areas, it IS INCLUDED in that set, so it IS one of those things. If anything IS NOT IN an area, it IS NOT INCLUDEDs in that set, so it IS NOT one of those things. So as we do Venn diagrams, think:

IS = IN an area
IS NOT = NOT IN an area

Now we can look at the 4 areas and figure out what they each mean with respect to the two sets we are looking at. For instance, if something were IN area 1, it WOULD BE a human (because area 1 is part of the circle representing humans). However, this thing is NOT in any of the areas making up the male circle, so it WOULD NOT be a male. So anything in area 1 would be a human, but not a male (like human females). To illustrate this, we will make a chart of each of the 4 areas:

Something in this area:	IS a human (is IN the human circle)?	IS a male (is IN the male circle)?
1	YES	NO
2	YES	YES
3	NO	YES
4	NO	NO

Each area represents a different combination of being a human and being a male. Area 1 represents human non-males (human females), area 2 represents human males, area 3 represents non-human males (like my male dog, Rover), and area 4 represents non-human non-males (like my car, which is not a human and it is not a male).

Now let's go back to the statement, "Some humans are males." Every categorical statement asserts a relationship between the two terms or sets in the statement. This statement is a particular affirmative, or I statement. It is telling us that PART of the set, humans is INCLUDED in the set, males. It is telling us that some things in the set, humans, are also in the set, males, or that some things are both a human AND a male. This allows us to focus on one particular area of the diagram, the area in which something would be a human AND a male. What area is that? Area 2. Notice that area 2 is IN the human circle, so it's a human, AND it's IN the male circle, so it's a male. But at this point we don't have any way of identifying what the diagram is supposed to represent, since all of the areas are open, which doesn't tell us anything. We are now going to start making marks on the diagram to represent the relationships expressed in the statements. Here's the chart of the marks again:

Mark	Meaning
X in an area	There is at least one of these things.
Shading in an area	The area is EMPTY – no such things exist.

Our statement is telling us that some (at least one) humans are male. We know we're interested in area 2 on the diagram. Now we have to put a mark, either an X or shading, in area 2. Which would we put? If "some" means "at least one" and an X means "at least one", then it would follow that an X in area 2 would represent "Some (at least one) humans are males." So that's what we'll do – draw an X in area 2:

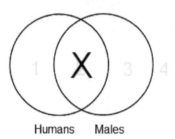

Humans   Males

This diagram now reads, "there is at least one thing that is a human and a male," which is the meaning of "some humans are males." Now, how about "some humans are not males"? This statements is asserting there is at least one thing that IS a human but IS NOT a male. So we have to look at the area in which something would be human and NOT male. Which area is that? Think; IN human and NOT IN male. That's area 1! Now we have to put a mark there to illustrate the meaning of the sentence. We know the mark has to go in area 1, and we know the sentence is only referring to SOME humans, which means "at least one," so we can conclude that the mark to use is an X. We place an X in area 1:

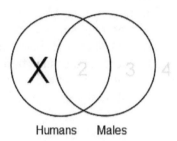

Humans   Males

Now let's try the E statement, the universal negative. In order to work with a true statement, I'm going to change the predicate to "fish." So we have "No humans are fish." In other words, this statement asserts that nothing is a human and a fish. That means that the area on the diagram in which something would be a human and a fish must be empty, or have nothing in it. So we have to identify again the area in which something would be both a human and a fish. That's area 2. Now we have to place a mark of some sort there. If we put an X there it would illustrate "some humans are fish" but that's not what we want. We want "NO humans are fish. Our other mark is shading. Shading means "there are no such things." This is precisely what our statement is telling us – there are no human-fishes. So if we put shading in area 2, we will have illustrated the meaning of the statement:

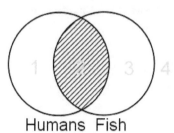

Humans Fish

The final categorical statement form is the most common, but has the most difficult diagram. The form, as we have seen, is "All S are P" and the example we have seen is "All humans are mammals." We could put a circle in a circle as we did at first, but that method won't work for evaluating categorical arguments. We have to try to illustrate "All humans are mammals" in the two-circle diagram format we are using. We can only use an X or shading on the diagram. An X means "at least one" or "some", but our statement is universal, not particular. We used shading for the E statement, which is a universal. All of that seems to imply that we need to use shading to do the A statement. Shading implies an area where no things exist, so if all humans are mammals, which area on the diagram would not have anything in it? Area 2 is humans that ARE mammals, so that has things in it. Area 3 is mammals that aren't human, and there are lots of those, so Area 3 can't be shaded. Let's look at area 1. Something in area 1 would be a human, but NOT a mammal. Are there any such things? Not if all humans are mammals! So we can say that if all humans are mammals, area 1 must not have anything in it, so it must be shaded. Here is what it looks like:

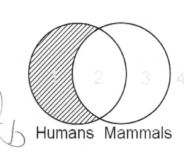

Humans Mammals

Think of the shading as herding or corralling all the humans into the mammal circle – if anything is a human, it must be in the mammal circle, which is area 2. Area 1 must be empty.

Now we are prepared to construct a chart of the four categorical statement forms, with their letters and diagrams. **It is VITAL that you know these 4 statement forms and their diagrams VERY WELL before we continue. The rest of the section on Categorical Logic depends on these 4 forms and their diagrams. Practice, practice, practice!**

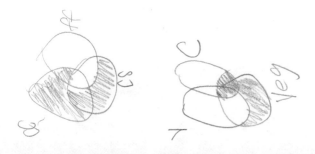

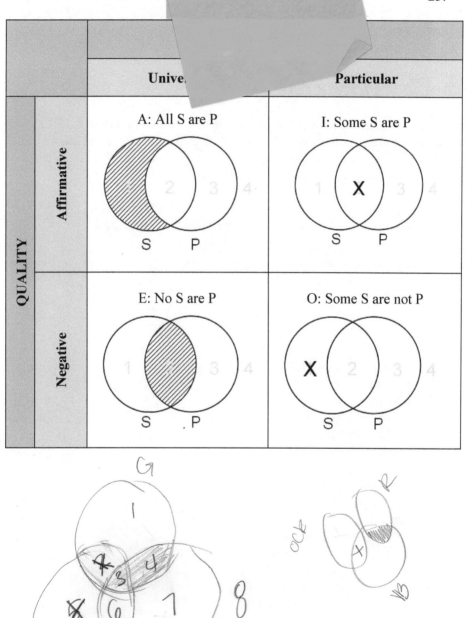

		Unive...	Particular
QUALITY	**Affirmative**	A: All S are P	I: Some S are P
	Negative	E: No S are P	O: Some S are not P

Exercises

If you cannot do ALL of these statements without error, you need to keep working on them before you move on. YOU MUST BE ABLE TO DIAGRAM STATEMENTS TO PROCEED FROM HERE!

Draw the diagram of each of the following statements. You must LABEL your circles. By convention, use a capital letter for each term and put the Subject term on the left and the Predicate term on the right. We don't care at this point whether the statements are true or false.

Example: Some birds are loud animals.
B = birds (subject), L = Loud animals (predicate): Some B are L

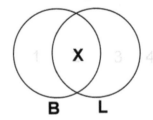

1. All dogs are mammals.
2. No dogs are fish.
3. No fish are dogs.
4. Some dogs are Labrador retrievers.
5. All Labrador retrievers are dogs.
6. Some dogs are NOT Labrador retrievers.
7. Some children are adorable.
8. Some children are NOT adorable.
9. Some adorable things are children.
10. Some adorable things are NOT children.
11. All firefighters are brave people.
12. No firefighters are cowards.
13. Some firefighters are men.
14. Some firefighters are women.
15. Some firefighters are not men.
16. Some firefighters are not women.
17. All presidents of the U.S. are American citizens (terms: presidents of the U.S. and American citizens).
18. Some American citizens are presidents of the U.S.
19. No French citizens are presidents of the U.S.
20. No presidents of the U.S. are French citizens.
21. All residents of southern California are people who live in earthquake zones.

22. Some people who live in earthquake zones are residents of southern California.
23. Some people who live in earthquake zones are not residents of southern California.

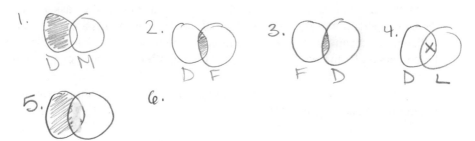

2.3 – Operations on Categorical Statements

Conversion

The Medieval Latin philosophers were very interested in categorical statement and studied them carefully. One of the questions they asked was, "What happens if we start to move the parts of the statements around? Will it change the meaning?" One of the most common ways this happens is with the universal affirmative (A) statement. People often think they can switch the subject and predicate term around and end up with a statement that means the same thing. In fact, this is one of the most common errors in reasoning that humans make. Consider this example:

1.   All dogs are mammals. ✓
2.   All mammals are dogs. ✗

In this case, the first statement is true, but the second statement is false (horses, elephants, etc., are mammals but aren't dogs). So they can't *mean* the same thing! One way to demonstrate that they don't mean the same thing is to draw Venn diagrams for each of the statements and compare them. The Venn diagram for "All dogs are mammals" is:

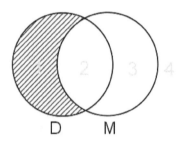

D   M

To compare the Venn diagram for "All mammals are dogs", we have to keep D on the left and M on the right (two diagrams have to be labeled exactly the same way to be compared). Now, to diagram "All mammals are dogs," we would have to fill in the M circle outside of D (If it's a mammal, then it's a dog, so nothing can be a mammal without being a dog). So the diagram would be:

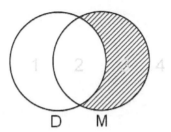

D   M

The rule for comparing diagrams is, "Same diagram = same meaning; different diagram = different meaning." As we intuited, these two statements have different meanings, and the diagrams show or illustrate the difference in meaning.

The act of changing the structure of a categorical statement is called an *operation*. The particular operation of switching the subject and predicate terms is called "Conversion." In addition to the A statement, conversion can be performed on any of the other statement forms as well.

For instance, take the E statement, "No dogs are fish." The diagram for that statement is:

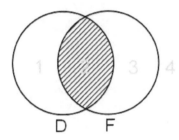

D   F

What happens if we "convert" the statement? To do that, we switch the subject and predicate term. It becomes "No fish are dogs." Notice that these statements are both true. That doesn't guarantee that they mean the same things, but at least it's not ruled out. To test, we can draw a Venn diagram of the new statement, keeping D and F on the same sides as in the original diagram. This, time, we have to diagram that there are no things that are both fish (Fs) and dogs (Ds). Where would something be both an F and a D? In area 2. So area 2 must be empty, so we shade area two:

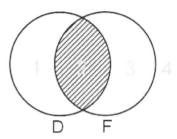

Now compare the two diagrams. They are exactly the same. Remember the rule: same diagram = same meaning; different diagram = different meaning. In this case, the statement and its converted form have the same meaning.

Let's try conversion on an I statement. Consider "Some presidents are males." The diagram would be:

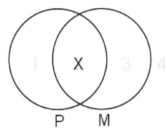

Now we convert the statement. It becomes "Some males are presidents." This statement is telling us that there is at least one thing that is a male and a president. Its diagram would be (keeping P on the left and M on the right):

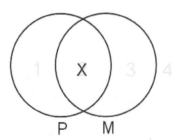

The diagrams are the same, so the statements mean the same thing. If you think about it, if some presidents are males, it would follow that some males are presidents (the presidents who are males would be males who are presidents!).

Finally, we look at the O statement. Consider "Some humans are not bankers." The diagram would be:

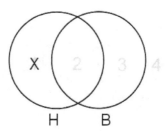

Next, convert the statement. The new statement is "Some bankers are not humans." Like the A statement, the first statement was true, but this one is false. That means they can't mean the same thing. The new statement says that there is at least one thing that is a banker, but is not a human. Something in area 3 would be a banker but not a human, so we put an X there. Here is the diagram (remember to keep the labels the same!).

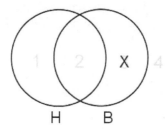

As we predicted, the diagram of "Some bankers are not humans" is different than the diagram of "Some humans are not bankers."

Obversion

The next operation is again one that most people are familiar with. Think of the sentence, "All dogs are not cute animals." This is an ambiguous sentence. It might mean "Some dogs are not cute animals" or it might mean, "No dogs are cute animals." Here we are interested in the second possibility. It seems that "All dogs are not cute animals" might mean, "No dogs are cute animals." But these statements have very different forms! Let's look at them more closely.

To get from (going the other direction) "No dogs are cute animals" to "All dogs are not cute animals," two operations have to occur. "No" has to become "all" and "cute animals" has to become "not cute animals." In the first operation, the QUALITY of the statement has changed. That is, it has changed from a universal negative (E) statement to a universal affirmative (A) statement. The quantity, universal, has stayed the same. But the quality has changed from negative to affirmative.

The second step is a bit more complicated. "Cute animals" has changed to "not cute animals." In order to understand this step, we must learn about *class complements* or *set complements*. The *complement* of a class or a set is the set of everything that is NOT in the original set. This sounds very abstract, but think of the circles we are using for sets or classes or terms. When we draw a circle to represent "cute dogs," we can think of everything that is NOT in that circle. That would be the set of everything that is NOT a cute dog. Another way of referring to this set is "non-cute-dogs." What we have done in the statement above is replaced a set, "cute dogs" with its *complement* "non-cute-dogs" (although it was written informally as "not cute dogs").

The operation we are considering here is called "obversion." To summarize, it involves these two steps:

1. Change the quality (positive to negative; negative to positive).
2. Replace the predicate term with its complement (more simply, replace "P" with "non-P").

Now, let's go through the operation with the four statement types. First, "All dogs are mammals." The diagram would be:

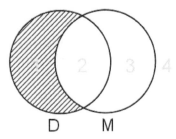

D   M

We obvert the statement. It's helpful to do it in steps:

1. Change the quality. It's a universal affirmative, so it becomes a universal negative; "No dogs are mammals."
2. Replace the predicate term with its complement. The predicate term is "mammals." It becomes "non-mammals" and the statement becomes:

No dogs are non-mammals.

To diagram the statement, we have to think through what it means. Remember, we have to label the diagram in just the same way as the first one. So we have to use "D" on the left for "dogs" and "M" on the right for "mammals" (even though our statement now has "non-mammals"). "No dogs are non-mammals" means that there are not any dogs that are non-mammals, or not any dogs that are not mammals. In terms of the diagram, this means that there are no dogs that are not in the mammal circle. Area 1 would be where dogs would be not in the mammal circle, so we know there is nothing in that area, so we shade area 1.

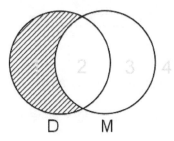

Compare the diagrams. They are both shaded in area 1, in the D circle that's outside of the M circle. The diagrams are the same and the statements mean the same thing.

The E statement was done as the opening illustration. We'll repeat it here with "No dogs are fish." The diagram is:

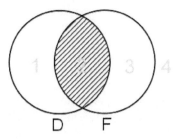

We obvert it:

1. Change the quality. It's a universal negative, so it becomes a universal affirmative; "All dogs are fish."
2. Replace the predicate term with its complement. The predicate term is "fish." It becomes "non-fish" and the statement becomes:

All dogs are non-fish.

Draw the new diagram, using D on the left and F on the right. The statement says, "All dogs are non-fish." That means that EVERY dog is NOT a fish, so there can't be any dogs that are fish, so nothing could be in area 2, so we shade it:

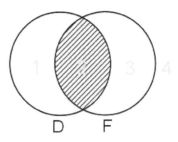

Again, the diagrams are the same, so the statements mean the same thing.

For the I statement, we start with "Some presidents are males."

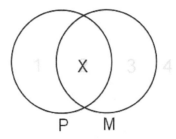

We obvert:

1. Change the quality. It's a particular affirmative, so it becomes a particular negative. Be careful on these. The particular negative form is "Some S are NOT P." You have to keep the NOT in there. It becomes "Some presidents are NOT males."
2. Replace the predicate term with its complement. The predicate term is "males." It becomes "non-males." Again, be careful. There is a NOT in the statement from step 1 and it has to remain there; the statement becomes:

Some presidents are NOT non-males.

In this case, the NOT non-males works like a double-negative in math; if something is NOT a non-male, then it is a male. So we end up with the statement we began with; "Some presidents are males"! Clearly this will have the same diagram:

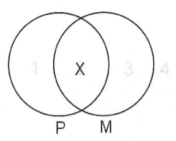

Finally, we must consider the O statement. We start with "Some humans are not bankers."

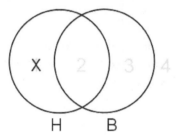

We obvert:
1. Change the quality. It's a particular negative, so it becomes a particular affirmative. Be careful. The particular negative form is "Some S are NOT P." You are making it affirmative; you have to drop the NOT. It becomes "Some humans are bankers."
2. Replace the predicate term with its complement. The predicate term is "bankers." It becomes "non-bankers." The statement becomes:

Some humans are non-bankers.

In this case, there is no practical difference between "not males" in the original statement and "non-males" in the obverted statement. So we end up with the same statement and the same diagram:

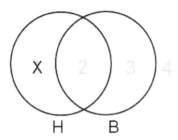

The interesting fact about obversion is that ALL of the statement forms, when obverted, yield a statement with the same meaning (you may not find this fascinating, but logicians do!).

Contraposition

The final operation we will consider is called contraposition. There is a reason that these three operations became well-known among logicians – I'll talk about it at the end, when we look at a chart of all of the operations. For now, we need to learn it. Contraposition, like obversion, is a two-step operation. Here are the steps:

1. Switch S and P. That is, do conversion on the statement.
2. Replace BOTH P and S with their complements ("P" becomes "non-P" and "S" becomes "non-S".

As we will see, drawing the diagrams becomes quite complex with these! Begin with the A statement we have been using, "All dogs are mammals." Its diagram, once again, is:

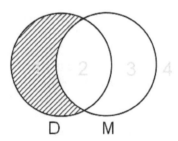

We contrapose it:

1. Convert: "All dogs are mammals" becomes "all mammals are dogs."

2. Replace both terms with their complements. "Mammals" becomes "non-mammals" and "dogs" becomes "non-dogs." The result is:

All non-mammals are non-dogs

The diagram for this statement is difficult. It must be labeled with D on the left and M on the right, just as the first diagram was. Now we have to mark it to show that all non-mammals are non-dogs. I will go through the conceptual process here; if you don't follow it (and I barely do!) just remember the result. The statement says, "If it's not a mammal, then it's not a dog." This means that there is nothing that is a non-mammal and a dog, or nothing is a dog but not a mammal. The area in which something would be a dog but not a mammal is area 1. So we know that area is empty and we have to shade it. So it becomes:

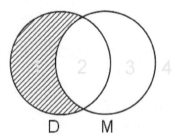

The two diagrams are the same! So, even though the wording of the statements seems very different, the relationship between the sets in an A statement and in a contraposed A statement is the same.

The E statement we are working with is "No dogs are fish."

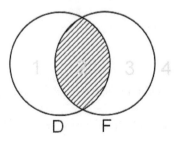

We contrapose it:

1. Convert: "No dogs are fish" becomes "no fish are dogs."

2. Replace both terms with their complements. "Fish" becomes "non-fish" and "dogs" becomes "non-dogs." The result is:

> No non-fish are non-dogs

Again, the diagram for this statement is very strange. If no non-fish are non-dogs, all non-fish are dogs (by obversion). That means that if something isn't a fish, it has to be a dog. So everything is either a fish or a dog! This is a very unusual claim – it means that area 4 is shaded! Here's what it would look like:

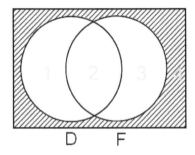

Clearly the diagrams are different.
The I statement is "Some presidents are males." Its diagram is:

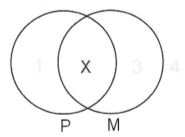

We contrapose it:

1. Convert: "Some presidents are males" becomes "some males are presidents."
2. Replace both terms with their complements. "males" becomes "non-males" and "presidents" becomes "non-presidents." The result is:

> Some non-males are non-presidents

This statement happens to be true (my wife, for instance is a non-male, non-president). But that doesn't mean that the two statements mean the same thing. To determine that, we need a diagram. If some non-males are non-presidents, that means that some things (like my wife) are neither males nor presidents. Where on the diagram would something be a non-male and a non-president? The circles represent presidents and males. A non-president, non-male would be outside both of those circles, or in area 4. So we place an X there:

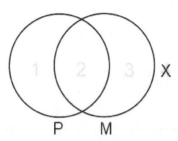

So, even though both statements are true, they don't mean the same thing, as illustrated by the diagrams.

Finally, there is the O statement; "Some humans are not bankers":

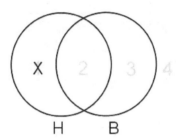

We contrapose it:

1. Convert: "Some humans are not bankers" becomes "some bankers are not humans" (remember to keep the NOT in the statement).
2. Replace both terms with their complements. "bankers" becomes "non-bankers" and "humans" becomes "non-humans." The result is:

Some non-bankers are not non-humans

This is another case where we have a double negative in the predicate. If something is not a non-human, then it is a human. So some things are non-bankers and are humans. That means something is outside of B and in H. That puts an X in area 1, just like the original statement.

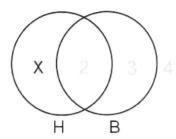

Now we can summarize all of the operations. Here is a chart with the basic forms across the top row, then a row for each of the operations. Operations that yield the same meaning are left; ones that yield a different meaning have large Xs through them.

Table of Operations on Categorical Statements

Standard form	All S are P	No S are P	Some S are P	Some S are not P
Conversion - Switch S and P	All P are S	No P are S	Some P are S	Some P are not S
Obversion - Change the quality - Replace "P" with "non-P"	No S are non-P	All S are non-P	Some S are not non-P	Some S are non-P
Contraposition - Convert - Replace "S" with "non-S" and "P" with "non-P"	All non-P are non-S	No non-P are non-S	Some non-P are non-S	Some non-P are not non-S

There are several interesting things in this chart. They have to do with certain symmetries between the statements. Notice for conversion, both A and O statements are different, while both E and I statements are the same. For contraposition, both A and O statements are the same, while both E and I statements are different. Notice also that both A and O statements have markings in area 1 (A is shading; O is an X) and both E and I statements have markings in area 2 (E is shading; I is an X). These symmetries don't have any special or particular meaning; they are just interesting to logicians, like symmetries in atoms are interesting to physicists or symmetries in strings of numbers are interesting to mathematicians. They can help you remember the way the operations come out, and can be useful in that sense.

Exercises

The following statements are followed by an operation. Draw the Venn diagram for the statement; perform the operation indicated; draw a diagram of the new statement, and say whether they mean the same thing or not (remember; same diagram = same meaning; different diagram = different meaning.)

1. All humans are things with hearts (Obversion)
2. Some humans are bald people (Conversion)
3. No children are good listeners (Contraposition)
4. Some children are artists (Conversion)
5. No ducks are geese (Obversion)
6. Some ducklings are ugly things (Contraposition)
7. Some ducklings are not ugly things (Contraposition)
8. All students are hard workers (Obversion)
9. All philosophers are intelligent people (Obversion)
10. All intelligent people are philosophers (Obversion)
11. No politicians are honest people (Conversion)
12. Some politicians are honest people (Conversion)
13. Some politicians are honest people (Contraposition)
14. Some politicians are not honest people (Conversion)
15. Some politicians are not honest people (Contraposition)

For even more practice, do ALL of the operations with each of these statements.

2.4 – Categorical Arguments

Now it is time to put together all that we have learned and talk about the point of Categorical Logic, categorical arguments. Remember this valid deductive categorical argument from the introduction?

>All *humans* are **mammals**.
>All *doctors* are *humans*.
>Therefore, all *doctors* are **mammals**.

This argument, like all categorical arguments, is composed of categorical statements. Categorical arguments always contain exactly 3 terms and each term appears exactly twice. The terms in the argument above are *humans*, **mammals**, and *doctors*. Note how each statement has two terms, there are three terms altogether in the argument, and each term shows up twice.

To help keep track of the terms, they have names. The two primary terms of the argument are the two terms in the conclusion (that's what you are being convinced of). The *subject term of the conclusion* is called the *subject term of the argument* (in this case, *doctors*). The *predicate term of the conclusion* is called the *predicate term of the argument* (**mammals**). The other term shows up in both premises, but not the conclusion (*humans*). This is called the *middle term of the argument*. The word "middle" comes from the fact that this term links together the subject term and the predicate term of the conclusion – it comes between them.

The validity of this argument is pretty intuitive. If all humans are mammals and all doctors are humans, then it should follow that all doctors are mammals. But some categorical arguments are much less intuitive. Consider this one:

>Some fruit are red.
>Some fruit are apples.
>Therefore, some apples are red.

This argument sounds valid, because all of the statements are true, including the conclusion. but in fact, it is invalid. We can use the system of Venn Diagrams to test arguments for validity in a systematic way and to show symbolically the validity or invalidity of categorical arguments. To do this, we have to expand our Venn Diagram from a 2-circle diagram to a 3-circle diagram.

Three-circle Venn Diagrams

Since there are three terms in a categorical argument, we have to find a way to symbolize and evaluate the relationships between all three terms. The Venn Diagrams we have used so far only have two circles, so they can only display the relationship between two terms. We will now add a third circle to the diagram, like this:

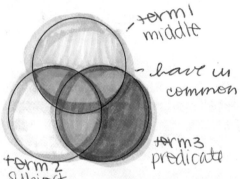

The third circle intersects each of the other two circles, creating areas of overlap for all of the different relationships for three terms or sets. Technically, any circle can represent any term from the argument, but there is a conventional way of assigning labels, and this will allow us to simply things later, so here is the conventional labeling system: The lower left circle is the SUBJECT TERM of the CONCLUSION; the lower right circle is the PREDICATE TERM of the CONCLUSION, and the top circle is the MIDDLE TERM. Like this:

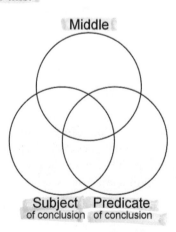

Middle

Subject   Predicate
of conclusion of conclusion

We can number the different areas and talk about the relationships they represent as we did for the two-circle diagrams.

A Formal Introduction to Critical Thinking

   Imagine that S stands for Salsa dancers, P stands for Polka dancers, and M stands for Macarena dancers. We will go through the same exercise as we did for the two-circle diagram, but now there are 8 areas to consider rather than 4. The rules, to repeat, are, if anything is IN a circle, it IS included in that set, so it IS one of those things. If anything IS NOT IN a circle, it IS NOT included in that set, so it IS NOT one of those things. So as we do Venn diagrams, think:

IN a circle = IS

NOT IN a circle = IS NOT

   We can look at the 8 areas and figure out what they each mean with respect to the three sets we are looking at. For instance, if something were IN area 1, it WOULD BE a Macarena dancer (because area 1 is part of the circle representing Macarena dancers). However this thing is NOT in any of the areas making up the Salsa dancer circle or the Polka dancer circle, so it WOULD NOT be either of those things. So anything in area 1 would be a Macarena dancer, but not a Salsa dancer or a Polka dancer. Here is the diagram of "something is in area 1."

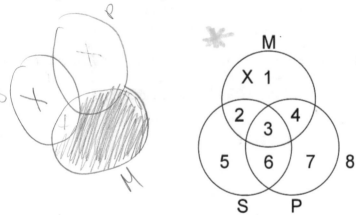

   We need to make a chart of the different areas. It might help you to draw a diagram and place an "X" in each of the areas to confirm what sets the individuals are in and not in. This chart shows ALL of the possible relationship for inclusion or exclusion from 3 sets.

Some-thing in this area:	IS a Macarena dancer (IN the M circle)?	IS a Salsa dancer (IN the S circle)?	IS a Polka dancer (IN the P circle)?
1	YES	NO	NO
2	YES	YES	NO
3	YES	YES	YES
4	YES	NO	YES
5	NO	YES	NO
6	NO	YES	YES
7	NO	NO	YES
8	NO	NO	NO

Diagramming Arguments

When we diagram arguments, we fill in the diagram with the same markings as we used for the two-circle diagrams:

1. An "X" in an area means "there is at least one individual in this area."
2. Shading in an area means "there are NO individuals in that area."

In addition, we will add these rules:

3. Always diagram universal premises before particular premises.
4. If one of the two areas of a larger area is shaded, then the "X" must go IN the other area (I'll explain this soon).
5. If neither of the two areas of a larger area is shaded, the "X" goes ON THE LINE between the two areas (I'll explain this soon).
6. ONLY DIAGRAM THE PREMISES! NEVER DRAW ANYTHING ON THE DIAGRAM FROM THE CONCLUSION!!!!

Rule 6 is VERY important. Breaking it is one of the most common errors that people make, and it will invalidate your diagram.

Example 1

Let's do an example to illustrate the process and the rules. We'll evaluate this argument:

All Poodles are Dogs.
Some Poodles are Cute animals.
Therefore, some Dogs are Cute animals.

First, identify the Subject, Predicate, and Middle terms of the argument. In this case, they are:

Subject term (Subject term of the *conclusion*): **Dogs** (D)
Predicate terms (Predicate term of the *conclusion*): **Cute animals** (C)
Middle term (Not in the conclusion):   **Poodles** (P)

I find it helpful to rewrite the argument using just letters for terms. This is especially helpful when the terms are long and complex. Here is this one rewritten:

All P are D.
Some P are C.
Therefore, some D are C.

Next, draw and label a Venn diagram with these three circles. Remember, technically, it doesn't matter which circle is which, so if you forget the pattern, don't worry. But I will always label the diagrams as Lower left = Subject, Lower right = Predicate, Top = Middle. It will help you immensely to always do the same:

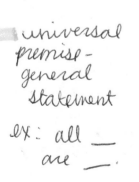

universal
premise -
general
statement

ex: all __
     are __.

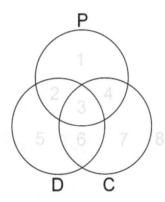

To diagram the argument, looking at the rules, we have to diagram the universal premise first; All P are D. I will illustrate this by starting with the two-circle diagram for the premise, then talking about transferring the information from the two-circle diagram to the three-circle diagram. I will always do this. If you become adept enough at drawing Venn diagrams, you can skip the two-circle diagrams and draw the three-circle diagrams directly.

The two-circle Venn diagram for "All P are D" is:

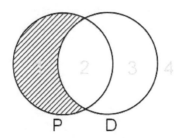

Now we have to imagine picking up the two-circle diagram and placing it on the three-circle diagram so that the P and D circles overlap the P and D circles on the three-circle diagram. The most important thing to remember here is that what is just one area in the two-circle diagram (area 1) will be TWO areas on the three-circle diagram (because the third circle cuts all the areas into two pieces). These two areas are marked in gray in the three-circle diagram. Area 1 in the two-circle diagram corresponds to areas 1 AND 4 in this three circle diagram. In terms of circles, the diagrams express the same relationship: Nothing is a P without also being a D. The area(s) in which something would be a P but not a D are areas 1 in the two circle diagram and areas 1 AND 4 in the three-circle diagram.

Here's what picking up the two-circle diagram and placing it on the three-circle diagram would look like:

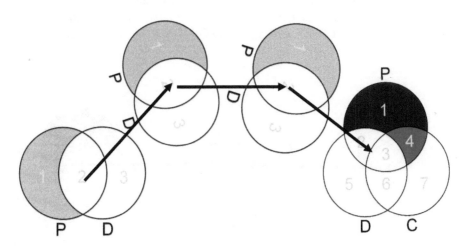

To summarize, we transferred the information for "All P are D" from the two-circle diagram (shading in area 1) to the three-circle diagram (shading in BOTH areas 1 AND 4). The information and the shading is the same (nothing can be a Poodle without being a Dog); the three-circle diagram is just more complicated than the two-circle diagram (there are two areas in which something would be a Poodle without being a Dog).

Now the first premise is diagrammed. We have to diagram the second premise, "Some Poodles are Cute animals" or "Some P are D." The process will be the same. We'll draw and look at the two-circle diagram and then transfer the information onto the three-circle diagram. The two circle

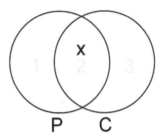

diagram is:

This diagram tells us that some (the "x" – at least one) Ps are Cs. Now we have to transfer this information onto the three-circle diagram. Imagine picking this up and setting it on the three-circle diagram:

Now, however, we encounter a problem. We know the X has to go in area 2 of the two-circle diagram – the area in which things are both P and C. That means that the X has to go in the area of the three-circle diagram where things are P and C. Which area is that? Well, it's TWO areas (remember, when we move from a two-circle diagram to a three-circle diagram we ALWAYS have to look at TWO areas). In which two areas would something be a P and a C? Areas 3 AND/OR 4. So the X has to go in area 3

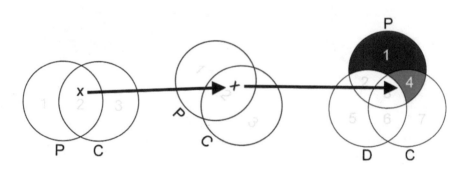

OR 4 (there's only one X). This is why we have rules 4 and 5 in our list of diagramming rules. They are:

4. If one of the two areas of a larger area is shaded, then the "X" must go IN the other area.
5. If neither of the two areas of a larger area is shaded, the "X" goes ON THE LINE between the two areas.

These two rules are about placing Xs. The "larger area" referred to in the rules is the area from the two-circle diagram which has now been divided into two smaller areas. In this argument we are looking at the larger area composed of the smaller areas 3 and 4. Would rule 4 or rule 5 apply to this argument? Area 4 is shaded, so rule 4 would apply. We KNOW there are NO INDIVIDUALS in area 4 – that's what shading means. So, the X must go in 3 OR 4, the X can't go in 4, so the X must go in area 3. So we place the X in area 3.

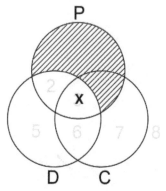

We have now diagrammed the two premises. Do we diagram the conclusion? NO!!! Remember rule 6 – NEVER DRAW ANYTHING ON THE DIAGRAM FROM THE CONCLUSION. We are done drawing the diagram. Now we EVALUATE.

Evaluating Arguments using Venn Diagrams

The Venn diagram shows us the logical structure of the argument. It shows us how the classes or sets in the argument are related to each other – all three of them. The question we must now ask is, *"Given the information that is supplied in the premises (and drawn on the diagram), would we know for sure that the conclusion is also true?* If the answer to that question is "YES", the argument is VALID. If the answer is "NO", the argument is NOT VALID or INVALID. The way we ask the question with respect to the diagram is, "Is the conclusion of THIS argument ALREADY diagrammed on

THIS diagram?" Again, "YES" means "VALID" and "NO" means "INVALID."

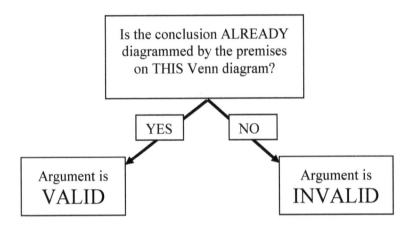

Let's return to the argument we've just diagrammed and evaluate it:

> All P are D
> Some P are C
> Therefore, some D are C

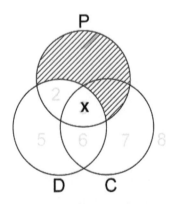

We ask: "is the conclusion ALREADY diagrammed on THIS diagram?" To answer the question, we have to think about what the conclusion says. An easy way to do this is to think about the 2-circle Venn diagram for the conclusion. Here it is (Some D are C):

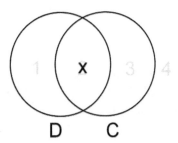

Next we ask, "do the D and C circles on the two diagrams show the same information?" In this case, the answer is "Yes." In more detail, the two-circle diagram has an X in area 2, in the overlap between the D and the C circles. That says that something IS a D AND a C. On the three-circle diagram, there is an X in area 3. But we know that anything in area 3 on the three-circle diagram IS a D AND a C. So in both cases, the X IS a D AND a C. So, given what we have on the three-circle diagram, we KNOW that something IS a D AND a C. The information from the premises of this argument has SHOWN us that the conclusion MUST be true. That is precisely what it means for a deductive argument to be valid. (If you are feeling confused because there isn't anything in area 6 of the three-circle diagram, read the footnote on this page. If you are not feeling confused about this, just continue on!)[4]

Example 2

Consider this argument:

predicate: end of conclusion
subject: beginning of conclusion

All <u>humans</u> are <u>mammals</u>.
All <u>women</u> are <u>humans</u>.
Therefore, all women are <u>mammals</u>. *middle: other term*

We will evaluate it for validity using a three-circle Venn Diagram.

1. Replace terms with letters:
subject: ~~mammals~~ women
predicate: mammals
middle: humans

---

[4]   The conclusion of this argument says, "Some D are C." Remember, "some" means "at least one." So to have the conclusion diagrammed means that there is *at least one* X in the overlap between D and C. Since there is an X in area 3, there is ALREADY an X that is a D and a C. That means we have all we need. The fact that area 6 has nothing in it is irrelevant. Remember, we have *at least one* X in the overlap between D and C.

All H are M
All W are H.
∴ All W are M[5]

2. Identify the Subject, Predicate, and Middle terms of the argument.
        Subject = W, Predicate = M, Middle = H.
3. Draw and label a Venn Diagram.

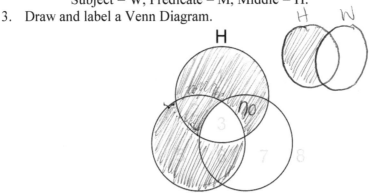

4. Diagram the PREMISES of the argument. As you become familiar
    with this method, you may want to diagram directly on the three-
    circle diagram. As you are learning, though, it is very helpful to
    draw the two-circle diagrams of the premises, which I will continue
    to do.
5. Diagram the UNIVERSAL premise first (since both of our premises
    are universal, it doesn't matter which you begin with – I will just do
    them in order).

    All H are M

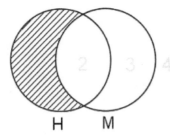

        We transfer this information onto the three-circle diagram.
    We have to shade all of the H circle outside of the M circle. Try to
    envision picking up the diagram and setting it on the three-circle

---

diagram. The areas on the three-circle diagram that are in H and outside of M are areas 1 and 2 (remember when you move to the three-circle diagram, you must always think about TWO areas). So areas 1 and 2 must be shaded.

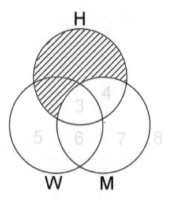

6. Diagram the second premise. In this case it is "All W are H." The two-circle diagram is:

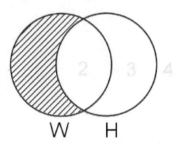

We now have to transfer this information onto the three-circle diagram. We have to shade all of W that is outside of H. That's area 1 on the two-circle diagram. Those would be areas 5 and 6 on the three-circle diagram. So;

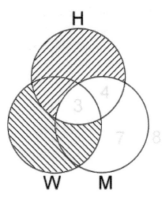

7. Evaluate the argument for validity. The question, again, is, "Is the
conclusion ALREADY diagrammed on this diagram?" To answer it,
we have to think about what the conclusion says. It says "All W are
M." To evaluate whether it is diagrammed on this diagram, we will
draw the two-circle diagram. (If you can answer the question without
drawing the two-circle diagram, that's great).

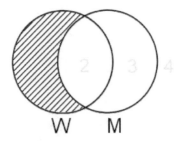

Is the information shown on the two-circle diagram already
shown on the three-circle diagram? The two-circle diagram shows
all of W outside of M (area 1) shaded. Is all of W outside of M
shaded on the three circle diagram? The areas that are in W and
outside of M are areas 2 and 5. Notice that they are both shaded (one
is shaded by one premise, the other is shaded by the second premise
– that's just fine). So all of W outside of M is shaded by the
premises. The conclusion is ALREADY diagrammed by the
premises. So the argument is VALID. (If you are feeling confused
about the fact that area 6 is also shaded in the diagram, read the
footnote – if not, don't worry about it!).[6]

---

[6] Some people are thrown off by the shading in area 6. But it is not relevant. Note
that the ONLY portion of the W circle left unshaded is area 3 – but that entire
portion is inside the M circle. So anything that is a W (woman) MUST BE an M

Example 3

All humans are mammals.
Some mammals are things with black hair.
Therefore, some humans are things with black hair.

We will evaluate this argument using a three-circle Venn Diagram.

1. Replace terms with letters:

All H are M   subject: humans
Some M are B.   predicate: black hair
∴ Some H are B   middle: mammals.

2. Identify the Subject, Predicate, and Middle terms of the argument.
Subject = H, Predicate = B, Middle = M.
3. Diagram the PREMISES of the argument. As you become familiar with this method, you may want to diagram directly on the three-circle diagram. As you are learning, though, it is very helpful to draw the two-circle diagrams of the premises, which I will continue to do.
4. Diagram the UNIVERSAL premise first (since both of our premises are universal, it doesn't matter which you begin with – I will just do them in order).

All H are M

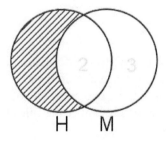

<hr>

(mammal). So all women are mammals, just like the argument concludes. The important point here is that no information in any area other than the two areas identified in the conclusion (areas 2 and 5 in this case) is relevant to the question of whether the conclusion is diagrammed.

We transfer this information onto the three-circle diagram. We have to shade all of the H circle outside of the M circle. This time H is the lower left circle and M is the top circle. We have to shade all of H outside of M, which would be areas 5 and 6.

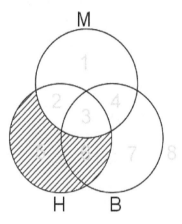

5. Diagram the second premise. In this case it is "Some M are B." The two-circle diagram is:

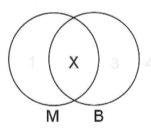

We have to transfer this information onto the three-circle diagram. We have to place and X in the area where M and B overlap. That's going to be two areas on the three-circle diagram. It's areas 3 and 4. Now remember the rules for placing Xs:

   4. If one of the two areas of a larger area is shaded, then the "X" must go IN the other area.
   5. If neither of the two areas of a larger area is shaded, the "X" goes ON THE LINE between the two areas.

In this case, there is no shading in either area 3 or 4. Rule 5 applies – we have to put the X in the larger area comprised of 3 and 4 but on the internal line dividing 3 from 4:

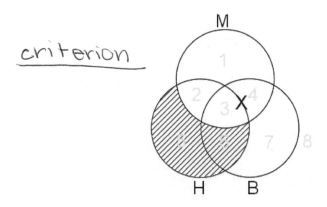

criterion

6. Evaluate the argument for validity. The question, again, is, "Is the conclusion ALREADY diagrammed on this diagram. This one is a little tricky. It says, "Some H are B." Now the question is, do we know that this is true (for sure) on this diagram? The answer is NO. We need an X in area 3 or 6 to know for sure that some H is B. There *might be* an X in area 3because there is an X on the line, but the criterion is stronger. We have to know FOR SURE that there is something that is an H and a B. Since we do not know for sure, we must declare the argument INVALID.

Exercises

Use a 3-circle Venn Diagram to evaluate the following categorical arguments for validity. Your answer should include the following 4 steps:

1. The conclusion would be diagrammed if (describe where an X or shading would have to be to have the conclusion diagrammed).
2. There is/is not (what was described in step 1).
3. The conclusion is/is not diagrammed.
4. The argument is valid/invalid.

For example:
1. The conclusion would be diagrammed if there were an X in area 3 or 6.
2. There is an X in area 3.
3. The conclusion is diagrammed.

4. The argument is valid.

NOTE: The answer to the question "Is the conclusion (already) diagrammed by the premises?" IS the answer to the question "Is the argument valid?" Diagrammed = Valid and Not Diagrammed = Invalid.

1. Some cats are good pets
    <u>All good pets are soft pets</u>
    ∴ Some cats are soft pets

2. Some cats are soft pets
    <u>All good pets are soft pets</u>
    ∴ Some cats are good pets

3. Some cats are soft pets
    <u>All soft pets are good pets</u>
    ∴ Some cats are good pets

4. All Dobermans are biters
    <u>No biters are good pets</u>
    ∴ No Dobermans are good pets

5. Some Dobermans are biters
    <u>No biters are good pets</u>
    ∴ No Dobermans are good pets

6. Some Dobermans are biters
    <u>No biters are good pets</u>
    ∴ Some Dobermans are not good pets

7. Some Dobermans are not biters
    <u>No biters are good pets</u>
    ∴ Some Dobermans are good pets

8. Some Dobermans are not biters
    <u>All biters are poor pets</u>
    ∴ Some Dobermans are not poor pets

9. Some Dobermans are not biters
    <u>All poor pets are biters</u>
    ∴ Some Dobermans are not poor pets

10. Some Dobermans are biters
    Some biters are good pets
    ∴ Some Dobermans are good pets

11. Some horses are black things
    Some things in California are black things
    ∴ Some horses are things in California

12. All BMWs are fast cars.
    Some BMWs are not safe cars.
    ∴ Some safe cars are not fast cars.

13. No television shows are things that promote children's imaginations.
    Some television shows are things that claim to promote children's imaginations.
    ∴ Some things that claim to promote children's imaginations are not things that promote children's imaginations.

14. Some American politicians are people who take bribes.
    No people who take bribes are people that should be leaders of a democracy.
    ∴ Some people that should be leaders of a democracy are not American politicians.

15. All people who watch Lost are people who believe in the paranormal.
    All people who watch Lost are people who believe in time travel.
    ∴ All people who believe in time travel are people who believe in the paranormal.

16. All people who want to protect helpless animals are caring people.
    All people who want to protect fetuses in mothers' wombs are caring people.
    ∴ All people who want to protect helpless animals are people who want to protect fetuses in mothers' wombs.

17. All corporations are things that want to control the political process through advertising.
    All things that want to control the political process through advertising are things that want to undermine democracy.
    ∴ All corporations are things that want to undermine democracy.

18. All countries that have universal health care are advocaters of socialism.
    <u>No advocaters of socialism are admired by the United States.</u>
    ∴ No countries that have universal health care are admired by the United
    States

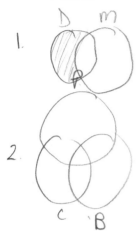

2.5 – Applications of Categorical Logic

Categorical statements and categorical syllogisms are part of our everyday logical analysis of the world. A strong case can even be made that ALL statements and ALL arguments can be analyzed using categorical logic. This is a very strong claim, and it shows that categorical logic is a very fundamental part of human reason. In this section we will look at some places in common life that categorical logic comes into play. The forms may seem strange here, but they really are everyday forms of argumentation and we use these concepts every day.

One additional technical approach to categorical syllogisms is helpful in this section. As you become familiar with doing categorical syllogisms, you may notice certain patterns in the way the syllogisms come out. These are well-documented patterns and they are shown in the following list of "General Rules for Categorical Syllogisms."

General Rules for Categorical Syllogisms

	If an argument has:	Then:
1.	A NEGATIVE premise	If valid, it can only have a NEGATIVE conclusion
2.	A PARTICULAR premise	If valid, it can only have a PARTICULAR conclusion
3.	2 NEGATIVE premises	It CANNOT be valid
4.	2 PARTICULAR premises	It CANNOT be valid
5.	2 UNIVERSAL premises	If valid, it can only have a UNIVERSAL conclusion
6.	2 AFFIRMATIVE premises	If valid, it can only have an AFFIRMATIVE conclusion

Enthymemes

Enthymemes with missing conclusions

The Greek philosopher, Aristotle, did a lot of thinking about categorical syllogisms. One common pattern that he recognized was a categorical argument in which some information was missing or unstated. For instance, if I'm looking at a floral display, and I say, "All roses are beautiful flowers, and some of the flowers in that display are roses," I am in fact presenting a categorical argument. But this argument only has two statements, while a proper categorical argument must have exactly two premises and one conclusion. Something is missing. Aristotle called this kind of argument an "enthymeme", which is the Greek word for "hole." Enthymemes are incomplete categorical arguments. They can only work if the missing part is supplied (and even then they may not work). We understand categorical arguments well enough intuitively that we can usually supply what's missing without thinking about it too much, as in this example about horses. But sometimes we can't tell intuitively what's missing. There is a process that we can use to formalize and evaluate enthymemes. Let's look at the enthymeme about flowers more closely. First, I will look at each statement and the word connecting them together:

All roses are beautiful flowers *∴ some beautiful*
(and) *flowers are in the*
Some of the flowers in that display are roses *display*
∴ all flowers are beautiful

Most people can guess that what's missing is something about the roses in that display being beautiful flowers. But we want to figure it out more precisely. The first step is to figure out what's missing. Ask yourself, "is what I have here 2 premises with an unstated conclusion or a premise and a conclusion, with another unstated premise?" (these are the only two possibilities).

The way to answer this is to think about whether what you have is one statement that is supposed to imply or support the truth of the other statement (this is what *inference* means), or whether the two statements are working together to imply or support something else. One quick way to answer this question is to look for indicator words. For our purposes, there are only two indicator words to look for: *and* and *because*. If two statements are joined by "and", they are both premises; if two statements are joined by "because", they are a conclusion (the FIRST statement) and a premise (the SECOND statement).

Indicator words

If the connecting word is	Then you have	And
And	Two premises	Both statements are premises
Because	A premise and conclusion	The FIRST statement is the conclusion; the SECOND statement is the premise.

Our argument has the indicator word "and", so we have two premises. We will now write them out in the form of a categorical argument, leaving a blank space for the conclusion. I will also write them with letters for the terms; often it is easier to do these by getting rid of complicated terms and just writing the statements with letters:

1.

All roses (R) are beautiful flowers (B)	All R are B
Some of the flowers in that display (F) are roses (R)	Some F are R

Now we have to work out what the conclusion is. Here are some observations that we can make about the argument:

2. 1. The middle term of the argument is the term that shows up in both premises: it is "roses" (R).
   2. That means the other two terms must be in the conclusion; they are "Beautiful flowers" (B) and "The flowers in that display" (F).

In addition, if we know the general rules about categorical arguments, there are some further conclusions we can draw about the kind of statement the conclusion is:

3. One premise is a particular premise. Rule 2 says that if an argument has a particular premise, it can only have a particular conclusion. So the conclusion must be particular.
4. Both premises are affirmative. Rule 6 says that if an argument has two affirmative premises, it can only have an affirmative conclusion. So the conclusion must be affirmative.

We can now conclude that the conclusion must be a particular affirmative conclusion (that is, an I statement), using the terms "beautiful flowers" and "flowers in that display." There are only two possible such statements, based on which is the subject and which is the predicate. They are:

Some flowers in that display are beautiful flowers	Some F are B
OR	
Some beautiful flowers are flowers in that display	Some B are F

Look at the statement forms with the letters. This is an I statement. Remembering the operations, which operation represents the relationship between these two statements? It is conversion. And what do we know about conversion of an I statement? They mean the same thing! So, in this case, it doesn't matter which term is the subject and which term is the predicate (but be careful – sometimes it DOES matter!). So we have in fact derived our conclusion: it is EITHER "Some B are F" or "Some F are B."

The enthymeme we have here can be completely analyzed and solved using the rules. But sometimes it's not so easy to solve them. A good practice is to draw a Venn diagram of the argument to validate your answer. Here is what the Venn diagram of these two premises would look like:

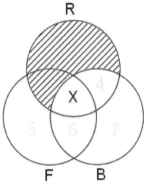

When it comes to evaluating arguments using Venn diagrams, all we diagram is the premises anyway, so for an enthymeme that's missing the conclusion, all you have to do is read the conclusion that is diagrammed on the diagram. Since we know that the conclusion has to do with the F and the B circles, we can just ask what we know about their relationship. There is an X in area 3; that X is in both the F and the B circles, so it's both an F and a B. So we know that at least one thing (the X) is an F and an B. The categorical statement for that relationship is "Some F are B." Since the X is in both circles, though, we know both that "Some F are B" and/or that "Some B are F," as we noted before we drew the diagram.

Enthymemes with missing premises

As I've said, many enthymemes, especially ones with missing conclusions, are easy to figure out intuitively. But many other enthymemes, especially ones with missing premises, are very difficult to figure out intuitively. This is actually why many enthymemes are used – they are a kind of trick to get you to believe something without stating it overtly. Very often what's left out is something that is controversial or that the arguer thinks you might not accept. Consider this argument:

All abortions are morally wrong because all murders are morally wrong.

The two statements are:

All abortions are morally wrong – *premise*
(because)
All murders are morally wrong – *conclusion*

The word "because" connecting the statements is our other indicator: A statement followed by "because" is always a conclusion – the word "because" means, "and this is the evidence to support the previous statement." So, any time you have two statements joined by "because," you have a conclusion and a premise with a premise missing. Now we can rewrite the statements in an argument form, leaving a "hole" where a premise should go:

All murders are morally wrong	All M are W
———————————————	*all A are M*
All abortions are morally wrong	All A are W

Be careful here; remember, the conclusion is the FIRST statement, so it is written UNDER the other statement when you rearrange them. Now we can start to look at this argument as a categorical argument. Here are some observations you can make:

1. The subject term of the argument (the subject term of the conclusion) is "Abortions" (A).
2. The predicate term of the argument (the predicate term of the conclusion) is "Morally wrong things" (W)
3. The middle term is the term that doesn't show up in the conclusion; "Murders" (M).

   Using the rules for categorical syllogisms, we can also deduce:

4. The conclusion is a universal. That means that BOTH premises have to be universal (because the only way to have a universal conclusion is to have two universal premises).
5. The conclusion is affirmative. That means that BOTH premises have to be affirmative (because the only way to have an affirmative conclusion is to have two affirmative premises).
6. Putting all of this together, we conclude that the missing premise must be a universal affirmative statement using the terms "Abortions" (A) and Murders (M). Keep in mind that we don't know which is the subject term of this statement and which is the predicate term, so there are two possibilities:

A. All abortions are murders (All A are M) OR

B. All murders are abortions (All M are A)

In this case, although it might be true that all abortions are murder, it is clearly not true that all murders are abortions, so you might have a tendency to prefer statement A to statement B. But you have to be careful; we are interested in the *validity* of arguments here, not *soundness*. So you have to go with which statement form makes the argument valid, even if the statement is not true. In this case, you might be able to work out intuitively which statement works, because this is a very familiar argument pattern. But to check it, I will construct a diagram using each of the statements. We are looking for the statement that makes the argument valid. Here are the diagrams:

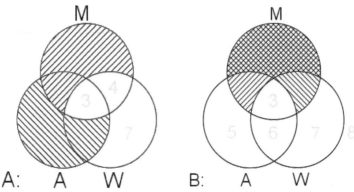

Diagram A is a valid argument; the conclusion is properly diagramed; diagram B is not a valid argument – no valid conclusion is diagramed there. So, we must take statement A as being the correct statement to fill in the hole.

Let's return to the question of why people use enthymemes. This argument shows one of the primary uses. Notice that the statement that was left out, "All abortions are murders" is very controversial. Some people think all abortions are murders and some don't think so. So the arguer has left out the controversial bit of evidence, evidently hoping that the listener would associate his or her feelings about murder with his or her feelings about abortions. Whichever side of the abortion debate you favor, this is a bad argument; you have not been given all of the evidence you need to evaluate it fully. As it turns out, the argument (when completed) is valid, but its soundness depends on your views about abortion.

Exercises

For the following enthymemes:
1. Identify whether a conclusion or a premise is missing.
2. Write out the argument in the correct order, using letters for terms.
3. Draw a Venn diagram(s) to complete the missing premise or conclusion. (You may and should use the rules to identify them as well, but you don't have to list those and you MUST still draw Venn diagrams).
4. Identify clearly the statement you are supplying to fill the hole.

Exercises
1. All children are adorable people and some children are funny people.
2. No fish are air-breathers and all salmon are fish.
3. All Republicans are critics of health care reform and some Californians are Republicans.
4. No Republicans are correct thinkers about health care and Bob is a Republican. (Translate "Bob is a Republican" as "All B are R" – "All things that are this person Bob are Republicans").
5. All dogs have hair because all dogs are mammals.
6. Some mammals are black because some dogs are black.
7. All happy children are well-fed children and some African children are not well-fed children.
8. Some Democrats are not capitalists because some Democrats are supporters of health care reform.
9. Some cars are not safe vehicles because no safe vehicles are recalled vehicles.
10. Some car companies should go out of business because they have caused the death of unsuspecting drivers.

1. premise
all a are a
some c are b
∴ some f are a
∴ some a are b

Sorites

The term "sorites" also comes from Aristotle. The Greek word "sorites" means "heap." A sorites is a categorical argument with more than two premises. A proper categorical argument, though, can only have two premises. So if there are more than two it is a problem. It is not a problem that cannot be solved, however. Consider this (somewhat non-sensical) argument:

No caustic people are decent people.
All aggressive people are belligerent people.
Some decent people are entertaining people.
All belligerent people are caustic people.
Therefore, some entertaining people are not aggressive people.

This is an argument made up of categorical statements, so it is a sort of categorical argument. The problem, again, is that we can only evaluate arguments of two premises, but this one has four. Here is a method for evaluating sorites:

STEPS

1. Replace all the terms with letters. This makes the process much easier.

    No C are D
    All A are B
    Some D are E
    All B are C
    Therefore, some E are not A

2. Reorder the premises:
    a. Find the premise that contains the PREDICATE term of the conclusion.
        i. In this case, that would be "All A are B."
    b. Make that the FIRST premise.
    c. Each NEXT premise will be the premise that contains the OTHER term from the previous premise.
        i. Since our first premise is now "All A are B," the next (second premise would the other premise that contains B, or "All B are C."
    d. Repeat step b until you have all the premises reordered.
    e. The other term in the last premise should be the SUBJECT term of the conclusion.

    i.   You started with the predicate term of the conclusion. Each statement is connected to the statements before and after it by having a term in common with them. So the last premise will be connected to the conclusion by having a term in common with it, the subject term.

All A are B
All B are C
No C are D
Some D are E
Therefore, some E are not A

(handwritten:) 1. predicate
2 – 3. middle terms
4. subject
5. conclusion

3.   Take the first two premises as an enthymeme with a missing conclusion. Derive the conclusion that follows from those two premises. Draw a diagram.

    a.   Our first two premises are "All A are B" and "All B are C." The diagram will be:

All A are B
<u>All B are C</u>

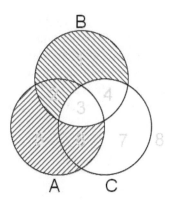

    b.   The conclusion that is diagrammed here must have to do with A and C. Areas 2 and 5 are shaded, which indicates that "All A are C."

Conclusion: All A are C

4.   Take the *conclusion you just derived* and now *treat it as a premise*. Pair it with the NEXT premise from the list, and derive the conclusion that follows from those two premises.

a. Our previous conclusion was "All A are C." That now becomes a premise. Our next premise is "No C are D." The diagram of these two statements would be:

All A are C
No C are D

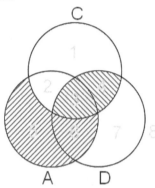

b. The conclusion that is diagrammed on this diagram is "No A are D."

Conclusion: No A are D

5. Repeat step 4 until you get back to the conclusion.

a. The conclusion of the previous step was "No A are D." We make it a premise and combine it with the next premise, "Some D are E." Notice that now we have two premises and a conclusion (Some E are not A), which is a proper categorical syllogism. Just write the conclusion underneath the two premises.

No A are D
Some D are E
Some E are not A

6. Use a diagram to verify that the conclusion follows from the last two premises.

a. Here is our final diagram:

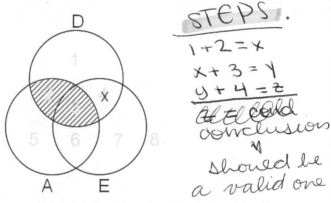

b. The diagram verifies that in fact, after all of these statements, "Some E are not A" does follow. So we have proven that the sorites as a whole is valid.

Exercises

Use the steps just outlined to solve the following sorites problems. Hint: These sorites are all valid; that is, they should all work out.

1) a) All carnivores are dangerous animals.
    b) All African lions are brave animals.
    c) All brave animals are carnivores.
    d) Therefore, all African lions are dangerous animals.

2) a) All children are entertaining individuals.
    b) Some artistic people are beautiful people.
    c) All beautiful people are people who deserve praise.
    d) All artistic people are children.
    e) Therefore, some entertaining people are people who deserve praise.

3) a) All dogs are animals.
    b) All Boeing 767s are jets.
    c) No animals are things made by humans.
    d) All jets are things made by humans.
    e) Therefore, no Boeing 767s are dogs.

4) a) All Democrats are people liberal about social issues.
    b) All people liberal about social issues are people who are in favor of abortion rights.
    c) Some people who are conservative about economic issues are people who favor increased government regulation of banks.
    d) No people who are in favor of abortion rights are people who are conservative about economic issues.
    e) Therefore, some people who favor increased government regulation of banks are not Democrats.

5) a) All go-getters are students.
    b) Some lazy people are underemployed people.
    c) No students are lazy people.
    d) All youthful optimists are go-getters.
    e) Therefore, some unemployed people are not youthful optimists

1. all c are i
    all i are h
    ∴ all c are h
    c

4. all c are l
    all p are l
    all c are p

2. all f are g
    some b are g
    some f are b

2. 3. all h are o
    some h are n
    some o are n
    h   o

Chapter 3: Sentential/Propositional Logic

3.1 – Introduction

[handwritten: What is Sentential Logic?]

Sentential Logic is another system of analyzing deductive arguments for validity. In this chapter we will learn the fundamentals of Sentential Logic, then we will apply them to more realistic and complex argument forms in Chapter 4, Natural Deduction. Both Sentential Logic and Natural Deduction employ a system of symbols to represent statements (and the arguments made of them), and a set of rules to manipulate and analyze the relationships between the statements (or, more specifically, between the premises and the conclusion).

3.2 – Simple Statements

[handwritten: What is the first step in analyzing argu.]

The first step in analyzing arguments in symbolic logic is to symbolize the statements that make up the argument. The basic rule for symbolizing statements is that a simple statement will be symbolized with a single capital letter. There are two ways to define "simple statement," a grammatical way and a logical way. Grammatically, **a *simple statement* is a statement that contains one subject and one verb and no connectives.** Logically, **a *simple statement* is a statement that contains no operators** (I will define "operators" shortly. The following are examples of simple statements: *[handwritten: Define a simple statement both gramatically and logically.]*

Bob ran.
Bob ran down the street.
Bob ran down the street last Saturday at noon.

[handwritten: What are the components of a simple statement]

Although these statements are of varying length and complexity, they all contain a single subject and verb ("Bob" and "ran", respectively), so they are all simple statements. Simple statements, again, are symbolized with a single capital letter. Any capital letter can stand for any simple statement, but it is helpful to choose a letter that reminds you of the statement it represents. For instance, we can symbolize any of the statements above with the capital letter, **B**.

The following statements are not simple statements:

Bob and Joe ran.
Bob ran and jumped.
Bob ran down the street and jumped into a waiting car.
Bob ran down the street, but Joe didn't go with him.

In each of these statements, there is either more than one subject (as in the first and the fourth), or more than one verb (as in the second, third, and fourth). They will each need to be symbolized by more than one statement letter. In addition to the simple statements in the statements above, there are words that *connect* the simple statements together ("and" in the first three, and "but" in the fourth). These words are called, grammatically, "connectives," and, logically, "operators." There is a limited set of such words in English (or any other language, for that matter). We will introduce symbols for these words as well. Once we have symbols for simple statements and the operators that we use to connect simple statements together, we can symbolize all English statements, no matter how complicated they are.

3.3 – Operators

What is an operator?

In Symbolic Logic, **an operator is a word or phrase that affects the truth value of a statement.** Remember, from our definition of "statement," that all statements have a truth value. We will say that the truth value of a statement is "T" if the statement is true and "F" if the statement is false.

Negation

Extra notes

The simplest operator is the negation. A note here is important: a simple sentence must always be in the *positive* voice. That is, "Bob is *not* coming" is NOT a simple statement, since it is negative. A simple statement in the negative is symbolized with a sentence letter for the (positive) statement, plus a "~" (called a "tilde"). So, "Bob is not coming" would be:

~B

where **B** stands for "Bob is coming."

"Not", then is an operator, since it acts on, or operates on, or changes, the meaning of a simple statement. There are some other expressions that are symbolized as a negation. For instance, "It is false that Bob is coming" and "It is not the case that Bob is coming" would also be symbolized as ~B. Think of the tilde like a "-" sign in mathematics – it's the *negative* of whatever it's attached to.

What is a tilde sign?

Conjunction

The next (and most common) operator is the conjunction. The most common conjunction is the word "and." We will use the symbol "**&**" to represent a conjunction. The following statements are conjunctions:

Bob ran and leaped.
Bob and Joe ran down the street.
Bob ran down the street, and Pete followed him.

The simple statements in the first statement above are "Bob ran" and "(Bob) leaped." We can use the letter **B** to symbolize "Bob ran" and the letter **L** to symbolize "(Bob) leaped." We would then symbolize "Bob ran and leaped" as

B & L

Similarly, if "Bob ran down the street" is symbolized as **B** and "Joe ran down the street is symbolized as **J**, "Bob and Joe ran down the street" would be symbolized as

B & J

Finally, if **B** symbolizes "Bob ran down the street" and **P** symbolizes "Pete followed him," then "Bob ran down the street and Pete followed him" would be symbolized as

B & P

Although "and" is the most common conjunction, it is not the only word that is symbolized with **&**. In fact, **&** is the default connector in sentential logic. It is used in every case except when one of the other connectors is specifically called for. The following connectors are always symbolized as conjunctions:

But
However
Moreover
Furthermore

How would you symbolize a conjunction?

← What words are used as conjunctions?

Disjunction

A disjunction is an either/or statement, and is symbolized with a ∨ (wedge). The statement,

(Either) Bob will go the store or Mary will go to the store

would be symbolized,

B ∨ M

what is a disjunction and how is it symbolized?

where B stands for "Bob will go to the store" and M stands for "Mary will go to the store."

Conditional

The conditional is the most difficult, but most important, operator. In its simplest form, a conditional is an "if ... then" statement, such as

If Bob goes to the store, (then) Mary will go to the store.

The symbol for a conditional is →. The preceding sentence would be symbolized as

B → M

what is a conditional and how is it symbolized?

The two parts of a conditional statement have special names. The part to the left of the symbol is called the ***antecedent*** (from the Latin for "comes before"). The part to the right of the symbol is called the ***consequent*** (meaning "comes after", like "consequences"). These terms will be used throughout this text, so it is important to learn them.

There are many English expressions that express a conditional relationship. For our purposes, I will only use "if...then."

in a conditional what is the antecedent and the consequent (draw and label)?

3.4 – Symbolizing Compound Statements

Now that we understand operators, we will use the logical definition of "simple statement." A simple statement is **a statement that contains no operators**. The only other kind of statement in logic is a compound statement: **a statement that contains at least one operator**.

The simplest compound statement is a negated simple statement. It is important to remember that a negated simple statement is NOT a simple statement, but a compound statement.

The following statements are all examples of negated simple statements:

Statement	Simple Statement	Symbolization
Bob did not go to the store	B = "Bob went to the store"	~B
It is false that I love chocolate	C = "I love chocolate"	~C
It is not the case that Bob sings	S = "Bob sings"	~S

What is a binary operator?

The rest of the operators are called ***binary*** operators. "Binary" means that they connect ***exactly two*** statements together (i.e., no more than and no fewer than two). Some statements contain a number of simple statements and operators, and we must learn a process for symbolizing them so their meaning is clear.

This issue also arises in mathematics. Consider the following problem:

2 + 3 x 4

This expression is ambiguous. That means that, on the surface, we don't know what order to perform the operations in. And the order of operations affects the outcome:

If we do the addition first, we get;

2 + 3 = 5; 5 x 4 = 20

But if we do the multiplication first, we get;

3 x 4 = 12; 2 + 12 = 14

So the order of operation affects the answer. We have rules in mathematics that tell us what order to do operations, but the other way we can indicate the order is with parentheses. If we want to do the addition first, we write:

(2 + 3) x 4

And if we want to do the multiplication first, we write:

2 + (3 x 4)

In logic, the operators work like mathematical operators. So the following statement is ambiguous:

Bob bought ice cream and chocolate sauce or peanuts

It might mean "Bob bought ice cream and chocolate sauce, OR Bob bought peanuts", or it might mean "Bob bought ice cream, AND Bob bought chocolate sauce or peanuts." In English, we usually use commas to indicate how things are grouped. The original sentence, with commas, would be one of these two statements:

Bob bought ice cream and chocolate sauce, or peanuts.
Bob bought ice cream, and chocolate sauce or peanuts.

If we were to symbolize the original statement as

(I = "Bob bought ice cream", C = "Bob bought chocolate sauce", P = "Bob bought peanuts")

I & C ∨ P

we would encounter the same problem as we did in the math example: we can't tell how the events (statements) are grouped. In symbolizations, we use parentheses to indicate grouping. The statement would be one of the two following statements, corresponding to the two English sentences above:

(I & C) ∨ P
I & (C ∨ P)

As we learn to analyze arguments through symbolizations, it is vital to learn to group the elements of compound statements correctly. There is a set of rules for grouping statements with parentheses. A statement that meets all of these rules is called a "*well-formed formula*", or a *wff*, for short.

what is a well-formed formula.

1. A *tilde* works only on single statements.
    a. The statement may be simple or complex, but a tilde is always only attached to (the left of) a single statement.
    b. Parentheses and brackets are required to display the order of grouping for complex statements.

c. The following statements are wffs (note that the tilde is always the left-most operator in the statement and if it is attached to a compound statement then it is outside of the parentheses):
   i) ~B, ~(B & C), ~[(B & C) ∨ ~(D → ~F)], ~~A
d. The following statements are NOT wffs:
   i) A~, A~B, A & (B~C)

2. The remaining operators are *binary* operators. They work according to the following rules:
   a. Parentheses are required to display the order of grouping for statements involving more than 2 statements and/or more than one binary operator.
   b. Each non-tilde operator must connect *exactly two* statements (whether simple or compound)
      i) The following statements meet this condition:
         A ∨ B, (A & B) → C, [(A ≡ B) & ~(C ∨ D)] → [(B & C) → ~A]
      ii) The following statements do NOT meet this condition:
         B &, ∨ B, & B ∨, B & C → D
   c. If there is more than one simple statement, it must be connected to the other simple statements by *exactly* (no more than and no fewer than) *one* non-tilde operator, which is placed *between* the statements.
      i) The following statements meet this condition:
         1. A ∨ B, (A & B) → C, (A ≡ B) → [(B & C) → ~A]
      ii) The following statements do NOT meet this condition:
         1. AB, A & B → C, &ABC, A~B

What are the rules about
binary operators?

Exercises

<u>Translation Exercises</u>

Translate the following statements in to symbolic form. Be sure to use parentheses to indicate grouping. Commas always show where a main break (and parentheses) goes.
You may use ANY unique letter for simple statements. In the answer key for this exercise I will use:

Mary sings = M
Bob dances = B
Carla dances = C
Don sings = D

1. Mary sings and Bob dances.
2. Mary and Don sing, and Bob and Carla dance.
3. If Mary sings, then Carla dances.
4. If Mary doesn't sing, then Bob dances.
5. If Don sings or Mary sings, then Carla dances.
6. If Don sings or Mary sings, then Carla dances and Bob dances.
7. If Don sings or Bob dances, then Mary sings but Carla doesn't dance.
8. If Don sings then Mary sings, and if Bob dances then Carla dances.
9. If Mary sings then Don sings, and if Bob dances then Carla dances.
10. If Mary doesn't sing then Don doesn't sing, and if Bob dances then Carla doesn't dance.
11. If Carla doesn't dance then Bob doesn't dance, and if Don doesn't sing then Mary doesn't sing.
12. If Don doesn't sing, then Mary sings and Carla dances.
13. If Mary and Don sing, then Bob and Carla both dance.
14. Mary sings, and, if Don doesn't sing or Bob doesn't dance, then Carla dances.
15. If Don doesn't sing and Bob doesn't dance, then Mary sings and Carla dances.
16. If Bob doesn't dance, then Mary sings and Carla dances; and Bob doesn't dance.
17. If Mary or Don sing, then Carla dances; and if Mary sings and Don doesn't sing, then Bob dances.
18. If, if Bob dances then Mary sings, then if Carla doesn't dance, then Don sings.

19. It is not the case that if Mary and Don both sing then Carla and Don both dance; however, if Mary doesn't sing and Don doesn't sing, then neither Don nor Carla dance.
20. If it is not the case that if Mary sings, then Bob dances, then it not the case that either Mary and Don sing or neither Carla nor Bob dance.

3.6 – Truth Values

As we learned when we learned the definition of "statement," a statement is a sentence that is EITHER true or false. This means that every statement has a *truth value*. Simply, if a statement is true, it has a truth value of "true", which we will symbolize with a capital T. Similarly, if a statement is false, it has a truth value of "false", or F.

The following statements have a truth value of T.

Montana is a state in the United States of America.
The sky is blue (to normal-sighted humans).
The moon orbits the earth.
Richard Nixon is a former president of the Unites States of America.

The following statements have a truth value of F.

The United States borders Egypt.
All humans have 3 heads.
George Washington was the president of the United States in the
    year 2000 AD.
The moon is made of green cheese.

What is the study of Sentential logic?

The study of sentential logic is the study of how the truth values of compound statements are related to the truth values of the simple statements and the operators that make them up. That is, if we know the truth values of the statements that make up a compound statement, then the truth value of the compound statement is determined by the logical operator that connects them. In other words, a compound statement that uses a particular logical operator will be determined by the truth values of the statements that make it up and some information about the operator itself. We now turn to learning how the truth values of compound statements are related to the operators that make them up.

3.7 – Truth Tables

Truth tables in logic are very similar to function tables in math. Some of you may be familiar with a function table, like this:

x	x+2
1	3
2	4
3	5
10	12

A function table reads, "if you start with this value (x) and perform this function or operation (add 2), then you get this result (x + 2)." The table shows a range of values for the starting value (x is a variable that can stand for any number) and the corresponding result of the function, or operation. Truth tables in logic look like and function exactly like function tables in math.

Another analogy for truth tables is input-output tables in computer programming. Here is an input-output table for the function (x + 2).

Input(x)	Operation (x + 2)	Output
1	1 + 2	3
2	2 + 2	4
3	3 + 2	5
10	10 + 2	12

A truth table is a table of inputs (truth values of simple statements), operations (operators), and outputs (truth values of compound statements). There are four basic truth tables. *what does a truth table do?*

Characteristic Truth Table for the Negation

Suppose we have the simple statement, and the corresponding letter symbol:

All mammals have hair = A

This statement is true; it has a truth value of "T". We could add this to the statement:

All mammals have hair = A = T

Now, suppose we *negate* that statement. To negate a statement, we add "not" in front of it. We would get this symbolization:

Not all mammals have hair = ~A
("A" stands for "all mammals have hair"; the tilde is added to the simple positive statement form)

The negated statement ("*Not* all mammals have hair") is false (because it is TRUE that all mammals have hair). It has a truth value of "F". We can add this to the statement:

Not all mammals have hair = ~A = F

Notice that, if we take the statement away and just look at the symbols we get this relationship:

A = T
~A = F

This tells us that if a statement (A) is true, then the negation of that statement (~A) is false. Now consider, "the moon is made of green cheese." This statement is false; it would have a truth value of "F".

The moon is made of green cheese = M = F

Negate the statement – if "not" doesn't work, use "it is false that." It becomes "it is false that the moon is made of green cheese," which is true ("T").

It is false that the moon is made of green cheese = ~M = T

Taking the written statement out, we have

M = F
~M = T

This tells us that if a statement (M) is false, then the negation of that statement (~M) is true. extra notes
We have shown that for any statement in general, if the statement is true, negating it makes it false, and if the statement is false, negating makes it true. We can symbolize this information, using our operator symbols, like this:

p[7]	~p
T	**F**
F	**T**

This chart or table tells us that for any statement, p, its negation (~p) is false, and if it's true, its negation is false. Note that the truth values, T and F, go under the *tilde* on the negated statement, not under the statement. This is because it is the *p* in the first case that is true, while it's the negation, ~*p,* that is false, and it is *p* in the second case that is false, while it's ~*p* that is true. We put the truth value under the operator to indicate the truth value of the *negated* statement, as opposed to the truth value of the statement that's being negated.

Since this chart reveals the truth value of any negated sentence, based on the truth value of the statement that is being negated, we call it the *characteristic truth table for the negation*.

Characteristic Truth Table for the Conjunction

Suppose we have the two simple statements,

Bob went to the store. (S)
Bob bought some milk. (M)

Now, suppose we connect these two statements as a conjunction:

S & M

As with the negation, the truth of the conjunction ("Bob went to the store and Bob bought some milk") is based on the truth values of the two statements that are conjoined. Intuitively, if it is in fact true that Bob went to the store and it is also true that Bob bought some milk, then it would be true to say "Bob went to the store and Bob bought some milk." We can begin setting up a truth table for the conjunction by recording this information.

S	M	S & M
T	T	T

This simple truth table tells us that if the statement S is true and the statement M is true, the conjunction S & M is also true (note that we put the

---

[7] "p" here is a statement *variable*. It can stand for ANY statement, no matter how simple or complex, positive or negative.

"T" under the operator, &, for the compound statement, as we put the truth value under the tilde on the truth table for the negation). But there are other possible truth values for S and M. They could each be either true or false. What if in fact, Bob went to the store, (S is true) but he didn't buy any milk (M is false)? Then if I were to say, "Bob went to the store *and* Bob bought some milk," my statement would be false. We symbolize this on a truth table as:

S	M	S & M
T	F	F

Similarly, if Bob didn't go to the store (S is false), but Bob bought some milk (M is true - maybe he bought some from his neighbor), then if I were to say, "Bob went to the store *and* Bob bought some milk," my statement would again be false:

S	M	S & M
F	T	F

And, if Bob didn't go to the store (S is false) and he didn't buy any milk (M is false), then if I were to say, "Bob went to the store *and* Bob bought some milk," my statement would definitely be false.

S	M	S & M
F	F	F

What is the general rule

We can say that, in general, a conjunction is true if BOTH of its conjuncts are true, and is false if either (or both) of the conjuncts is false. From this information, we can construct a *characteristic truth table for the conjunction.*   *for conjunctions?*

For any two statements, p and q, and their conjunction, p & q, the following relationships hold:

p	q	p & q
T	T	T
T	F	F
F	T	F
F	F	F

This table symbolizes the information that any conjunction is true only when BOTH the conjuncts are true, and is false in every other case. The table includes all possible combinations of truth values for any two statements (the two left columns), and the truth value of the conjunctions for each of those cases.

Characteristic Truth Table for the Disjunction

All of the operators have characteristic truth tables. If we have the two statements,

> Bob went to the store. (S)
> Bob went to a movie. (M)

We can combine them with "or" into the compound statement, "Bob went to the store or Bob went to a movie," which would be symbolized by the disjunction:

S ∨ M

The case in which Bob went to the store AND Bob went to the movie (they're both true) is a special case, so we will come back to it momentarily. Let's begin with the case in which Bob went to the store and Bob didn't go to a movie. In this case, if I say, "Bob went to the store OR Bob went to the movie," my statement would be true (since it only claims that at least one of the two things happened). So we would get this line on our truth table:

S	M	S ∨ M
T	F	T

Similarly, if Bob didn't go the store, but Bob went to a movie, if I say, "Bob went to the store OR Bob went to the movie," my statement would still be true (since, again, Bob did at least one of these two things). So we would have:

S	M	S ∨ M
F	T	T

However, if Bob didn't go to the store and Bob didn't go to a movie, then if I say, "Bob went to the store OR Bob went to the movie," my statement would be false:

S	M	S ∨ M
F	F	F

Now we return to the case in which both S and M are true. In normal English, the word "or" can have one of two senses. It can have an *exclusive* sense, by which we mean that one of two things happened *but not both*. However, "or" can also mean that one or the other *or both* of two things happened. This is called the *inclusive* sense of "or." In everyday English, people are fairly evenly divided in whether they intend the inclusive or exclusive sense of "or." In sentential logic, though, we will use the *inclusive* sense. The reason for this is that we can easily symbolize the exclusive sense of "or" if we need it, so we will take the broader sense of the operator for our general sense. So, in the case in which Bob went to the store AND Bob went to the movie, we will say the claim that Bob went to the store OR Bob went to the movie is true. So,

S	M	S ∨ M
T	T	T

The characteristic truth table for a disjunction, then, is (putting the case where both statements are true first, as is the custom):

p	q	p ∨ q
T	T	T
T	F	T
F	T	T
F	F	F

The thing to note about the truth table for the disjunction is that disjunctions are true on every line EXCEPT when both disjuncts are false. This general rule can be very helpful in solving sentential logic problems, so it is advisable to memorize it along with the truth table.

What is the general rule for disjunctions?

Characteristic Truth Table for the Conditional

A conditional statement is an "if...then..." statement. Take the two statements,

It is raining out. (R)
Bob carries his umbrella. (U)

and a conditional composed of them;

R → U
"*If* it is raining out (R), *then* Bob carries his umbrella (U)"

When we talk about truth values for conditionals, we usually talk about whether a situation *confirms* or *disconfirms* the conditional relationship. Suppose that on a particular day, it is raining (R is true), and Bob is carrying his umbrella (U is true). If I were to say "If it is raining out, then Bob carries his umbrella," my statement would be confirmed by the evidence, so we would say the conditional is true:

R	U	R → U
T	T	T

Now, suppose on a particular day, it is raining out (R is true), but Bob is NOT carrying his umbrella (U is false). If I were to say "If it is raining out, then Bob carries his umbrella," my statement would be *disconfirmed* by the evidence (since Bob is not carrying his umbrella while it is raining), so in this case, the conditional is false:

R	U	R → U
T	F	F

Next, suppose that on a particular day, it is not raining out (R is false), but Bob is carrying his umbrella (U is true). If I were to say "If it is raining out, then Bob carries his umbrella," it is hard to evaluate the truth of my statement, since it only refers to times when it IS raining! This situation is kind of tricky. The main logical point here is that the conditional statement does not say that Bob ONLY carries his umbrella when it is raining, it says that WHEN (IF) it is raining, he carries his umbrella. But there might be other occasions on which he carries his umbrella as well. Maybe it's hailing out today, or snowing, or there's a forecast for rain in the afternoon, or he has to get his umbrella fixed and is taking it to the umbrella store. The important thing is that this situation *doesn't disconfirm* the conditional – it still could be true that IF it was raining, Bob would have his umbrella. So, since this situation doesn't disconfirm the conditional, we will give it the benefit of the doubt and say it is true:

R	U	R → U
F	T	T

Finally, consider the situation in which it is NOT raining out and Bob is NOT carrying his umbrella. Again, this statement doesn't give us any

A Formal Introduction to Critical Thinking

information about whether Bob would have his umbrella IF it was raining. But, since the situation *doesn't disconfirm* the conditional, we will again give it the benefit of the doubt and say it is true:

R	U	R → U
F	F	T

The characteristic truth table for the conditional, then, is:

p	q	p → q
T	T	T
T	F	F
F	T	T
F	F	T

what is the general rule

The general rule for conditionals, from the truth table, is, a conditional is ONLY false when the antecedent (the statement on the left of the symbol) is TRUE and the consequent (the statement on the right side of the symbol) is FALSE. In every other case it is true. The condition is the most important of the operators, for reasons that will become evident later, so it is vital to know the truth table and the general rule for conditionals.

for conditionals?

Summary of Characteristic Truth Tables

The combined characteristic truth tables of the binary operators are presented below. It is important to note that ALL of Symbolic Logic (this section and the next section) are based on THESE tables. If you don't know these tables absolutely by heart from now on, you will fall behind very quickly.

p	q	p & q	p ∨ q	p → q
T	T	**T**	**T**	**T**
T	F	**F**	**T**	**F**
F	T	**F**	**T**	**T**
F	F	**F**	**F**	**T**

Draw truth table

3.8 – Partial Truth Tables for Compound Statements

Consider the following simple statements, and their corresponding truth values:

Statement	Symbol	Truth Value
The U.S. is south of Canada	C	T
The U.S. is south of Mexico	M	F
The moon orbits the earth	O	T
The earth orbits the sun	S	T
Elvis is alive	E	F
Justin Bieber is alive	J	T

Now consider the following compound statements made up of these simple statements:

1. The U.S. is south of Canada and the U.S. is south of Mexico.
2. If the U.S. south of Canada, then it is south of Mexico.
3. Either Elvis is alive or Justin Bieber is alive.

These statements would have the following symbolizations:

1. C & M
2. C → M
3. E ∨ J

We can construct a truth table to determine the truth value of any compound statement, if we know the truth values of the statements that make it up. To construct a truth table (using #1 above as an example);

1. Write the statement and put a line under it;

   C & M
   ‾‾‾‾‾

2. Place the truth values of each simple statements below it;

   C & M
   ‾‾‾‾‾
   T   F

3. Use the characteristic truth tables to determine the truth value under each operator (in this case there is only one – the &). In this case, the truth value of "C & M" is False, since that is the truth value

under the & truth table when one of the conjuncts is false. The truth value of the compound statement will be the truth value placed under the operator.

C & M
T **F** F

The truth tables for the other statements, respectively, are:

C → M
T **F** F
(the second line, where p is T and q is F, on the truth table for the → is "F")

E ∨ R
F **T** T
(the third line on the truth table for the ∨ is "T").

These examples, although compound, are still very simple. But statements in arguments can be very complex. Consider this one:

If the U.S. is south of Canada, then it is south of Mexico, but the U.S. is south of Canada and it is not south of Mexico.

The symbolization of this statement would be:

(C → M) & (C & ~M)

This statement has several operators and parentheses. To determine its truth, we must add some rules to those above:

1. Write out the statement and put a line under it;

(C → M) & (C & ~M)

2. Place the known truth values under each simple statement;

(C → M) & (C & ~M)
 T   F   T   T

3. Change the truth values for any ***negated*** simple statements;

(C → M) & (C & ~M)
T   F   T   TF
(Since M is false, ~M must be true)

4. Starting inside the most inside parentheses, and working within
    parentheses first, determine the truth value for each operator.

    a. (C → M) & (C & ~M)
        T **F** F   T **T** TF
        The truth value of (C → M) is F, since C is true and M is false.
        The truth value of (C & ~M) is true, since C is true and ~M is
        true (Note: the truth value at issue here is ~M, not M).

    b. (C → M) **&** (C & ~M)
        T **F** F **F** T T TF

        The truth value of the & in the middle is determined by the truth
        value of (C → M) (false) and of (C & ~M) (true), since those are
        the two statements that are connected by the &.

5. The truth value of the *statement* as a whole is the LAST truth value
    determined, under the top-most level operator (which is called the
    MAIN operator). In the case above, the & in the middle is the
    MAIN operator, and the truth value of the overall statement is F.

    Still using the statements and truth values provided, consider the
    truth tables for the following statements:

    (C ∨ M) & (E ∨ J)
    T T F **T** F T T

    Since C is true and M is false, (C ∨ M) is true. Since E is false and R
    is true, (E ∨ R) is true. Since (C ∨ M) is true and (E ∨ J) is true, the
    & in the middle (the MAIN operator) is true, and the whole
    statement is true.

    [(C → ~M) ∨ (~E ∨ J)] → (O & ~S)
    T T TF **T** TF T T **F** T **F** FT

In this case, given the basic truth value assignments, (C → ~M) is true, (~E ∨ J) is true, and (O & ~S) is false. Thus, [(C → ~M) ∨ (~E ∨ R)] is a disjunction, both of whose disjuncts are true, so it is true. The whole statement is a conditional (MAIN operator) that has a true statement on the left hand side (the disjunction) and a false statement on the right hand side (the conjunction), so it is false.

~[(O → S) → (~E & J)]

F T T T   T   TF T T

Note that if there is a tilde outside of the outermost brackets, it will be the MAIN operator and will reverse the truth value of everything inside the brackets. Here, the truth value of the conditional inside the brackets it true, but the tilde is the MAIN operator, so the final truth value for the whole sentence is false.

Exercises

Partial Truth Tables.

Translate the following statements in to symbolic form (these are the same as the earlier translation exercise). Then, assuming the following truth values for the simple statements, determine the truth values of each of the compound statements.

"Mary sings", "Don sings", and "Carla dances" are all TRUE.
"Bob dances" is FALSE.

1. Mary sings and Bob dances.
2. Mary and Don sing, and Bob and Carla dance.
3. If Mary sings, then Carla dances.
4. If Mary doesn't sing, then Bob dances.
5. If Don sings or Mary sings, then Carla dances.
6. If Don sings or Mary sings, then Carla dances and Bob dances.
7. If Don sings or Bob dances, then Mary sings but Carla doesn't dance.
8. If Don sings then Mary sings, and if Bob dances then Carla dances.
9. If Mary sings then Don sings, and if Bob dances then Carla dances.
10. If Mary doesn't sing then Don doesn't sing, and if Bob dances then Carla doesn't dance.
11. If Carla doesn't dance then Bob doesn't dance, and if Don doesn't sing then Mary doesn't sing.
12. If Don doesn't sing, then Mary sings and Carla dances.

13. If Mary and Don sing, then Bob and Carla both dance.
14. Mary sings, and, if Don doesn't sing or Bob doesn't dance, then Carla dances.
15. If Don doesn't sing and Bob doesn't dance, then Mary sings and Carla dances.
16. If Bob doesn't dance, then Mary sings and Carla dances; and Bob doesn't dance.
17. If Mary or Don sing, then Carla dances; and if Mary sings and Don doesn't sing, then Bob dances.
18. If, if Bob dances then Mary sings, then if Carla doesn't dance, then Don sings.
19. It is not the case that if Mary and Don both sing then Carla and Don both dance; however, if Mary doesn't sing and Don doesn't sing, then neither Don nor Carla dance.
20. If it is not the case that if Mary sings, then Bob dances, then it not the case that either Mary and Don sing or neither Carla nor Bob dance.

3.9 – Complete Truth Tables

In the previous examples, we knew the truth values for the simple statements that made up the compound statements. However, logicians often want to consider the possible truth values for statement *forms* when the values of the simple statements are not known. In order to do this, logicians use a *complete truth table* for a statement or set of statements. Consider the statement:

$$(A \& B) \vee (A \vee B)$$

We don't know the truth values for A and B (we don't even know what statements they stand for!). But we can determine, for *any* combination of truth values for A and B, what the truth value of this compound statement would be.

Constructing a Complete Truth Table

To construct a complete truth table, we have to consider all of the possible combinations of truth values for the simple statements in the table. Since each statement can have 2 truth values (T or F), there is a formula that will reveal how many possible combinations there are. One statement has 2 truth values (T or F). With two statements, say, A and B, each of the statements can be either true or false. So, A can be true and B true, or A can be true, and B false, or A can be false, and B true, or A can be false, and B false. That is, for each possible value for A (T or F), B can have either value (T or F). So, we have to multiply the possibilities for A by the possibilities for B, or 2 X 2, which gives us 4 possible combinations. If you recall the characteristic truth tables, which were truth tables for two letters, each has 4 lines, or combinations. We draw a table with these possible values like this:

extra notes

How do you find how many possibilities there are for a compound statement?

A	B
T	T
T	F
F	T
F	F

Note that on this table, under the A, we put two Ts followed by two Fs and under the B we put one T followed by one F, alternating. We will refer back to this pattern as our statements become more complex.

Once we have laid out the truth value combinations for the simple statements, we put the statement whose truth table we want to investigate on the line next to the simple statements. The truth table for the statement above will look like this:

A	B	(A & B) ∨ (A ∨ B)
T	T	
T	F	
F	T	
F	F	

Now, working across, we can enter the truth values for A and B. They come from the values under A and B on the left side of the table (the inputs). EVERY A must get the same truth value and EVERY B must get the same truth value. In the first row, both are true.

A	B	(A & B) ∨ (A ∨ B)
T	T	T T T T
T	F	
F	T	
F	F	

Once the truth values for the simple statements are entered, work out the truth value of the compound statement for that row:

A	B	(A & B) ∨ (A ∨ B)
T	T	T TT T T T T
T	F	
F	T	
F	F	

As each row is completed, move to the next row, get the truth values from the left, and work out that row.

A	B	(A & B) ∨ (A ∨ B)
T	T	T TT T T T T
T	F	T F F T T T F
F	T	
F	F	

A	B	(A & B) ∨ (A ∨ B)
T	T	T **T** T **T** T **T** T
T	F	T **F** F **T** T **T** F
F	T	F **F** F **T** F **T** T
F	F	

A	B	(A & B) ∨ (A ∨ B)
T	T	T **T** T **T** T **T** T
T	F	T **F** F **T** T **T** F
F	T	F **F** F **T** F **T** T
F	F	F **F** F **F** F **F** F

Once the truth table is completed, the set of truth values under the main operator (represented below by the box) is said to be the *truth table* for this statement. This particular statement is true in every case except when A and B are both false. That, in itself, is not very interesting. But we're learning a process that can tell us some very interesting things about sets of statements.

A	B	(A & B) ∨ (A ∨ B)
T	T	T T T **T** T T T
T	F	T F F **T** T T F
F	T	F F F **T** F T T
F	F	F F F **F** F F F

Suppose we have this statement:

(A → B) & (A → ~C)

Now we have three simple statements. How many possible combinations of truth values are there? There are two possibilities for A (T or F), two for B (T or F), and two for C (T or F). We have to multiply the possibilities: 2 X 2 X 2 = 8. There are 8 possible truth value combinations for 3 statements.

The relationship between the number of letters and the number of truth value combinations for truth tables is 2^n, where n is the number of simple statements. That means that every additional statement doubles the number of possible combinations, or the number of rows on the truth table. You can see that truth tables will become very large and unwieldy very quickly. This is one of their main limitations.

To complete the truth table for our current example, with 3 simple statements (A, B, and C), we begin by filling out the combinations for these statements. The standard (and most efficient) procedure is to begin with the right-most letter (C) and place alternating Ts and Fs under it, for however many rows are required (in this case, 8):

A	B	C
		T
		F
		T
		F
		T
		F
		T
		F

Next, move to the next letter to the left, and double the number of Ts and Fs that are repeated. In this case, we will put 2 Ts followed by 2 Fs, alternating, under the B.

A	B	C
	T	T
	T	F
	F	T
	F	F
	T	T
	T	F
	F	T
	F	F

Next, move to the next letter to the left, and again double the number of Ts and Fs that are repeated. In this case, we will put 4 Ts followed by 4 Fs, alternating, under the A.

A	B	C
T	T	T
T	T	F
T	F	T
T	F	F
F	T	T
F	T	F
F	F	T
F	F	F

This procedure can be repeated for any number of simple letters. That is, if there were a 4th letter, there would be 16 rows, and the left-most letter would have 8 Ts followed by 8 Fs, etc.

Now that the truth value combinations are completed, we can determine the truth value of the statement for each row, using the method we have learned. That is, place the Ts and Fs under the simple statements on each row, and compute the truth value of the complete statement on each row.

The *truth table for a statement*, when a complete truth table has been completed, is the set of Ts and Fs in the *column under the main operator* (here identified with a box).

A	B	C	(A → B) & (A → ~C)
T	T	T	T T T **F** T F F T
T	T	F	T T T **T** T T T F
T	F	T	T F F **F** T F F T
T	F	F	T F F **F** T T T F
F	T	T	F T T **T** F T F T
F	T	F	F T T **T** F T T F
F	F	T	F T F **T** F T F T
F	F	F	F T F **T** F T T F

Truth Table Patterns for Single Statements

Certain statements have notable truth tables.

Tautologies or Logical Truths

Note the following truth table:

A	B	A ∨ (B ∨ ~B)
T	T	T **T** T T F T
T	F	T **T** F T T F
F	T	F **T** T T F T
F	F	F **T** F T T F

The statement is true under every truth value assignment (every row on the truth table). Any statement that has this pattern is called a *tautology* or a *logical truth*.

Logical Contradiction or Logical Falsehood

Now, note this truth table:

A	B	A & (B & ~B)
T	T	T **F** T F FT
T	F	T **F** F F TF
F	T	F **F** T F FT
F	F	F **F** F F TF

The statement is false on every truth value assignment. Any statement that has this pattern is said to be *logically contradictory* or a *logical falsehood*.

Contingent Statements

A statement that is neither logically true nor logically false (that is, it has both Ts and Fs on its truth table) is said to be *contingent*.

Exercises

Full Truth Tables for single statements

Use a full truth table to evaluate the following statements. Determine whether each statement is a tautology, a contradiction, or contingent.

1. (A & B) & (A & ~B)
2. (A → B) → (A & ~B)
3. (A ∨ B) ∨ (~A ∨ ~B)
4. ((A → B) → C) & ~C
5. (~M & D) → (~B → ~D)

Truth Table Patterns for Sets of Statements

In addition to being interested in truth table patterns for single statements and, logicians are interested in truth tables for *sets* of statements. This interest is directly related to the analysis of the validity of arguments, because, if you remember, an argument *is* a *set* of statements. That means we can use truth tables to analyze arguments for validity, which is our overall objective.

Consistency

There is one pattern for sets of statements that we will discuss before looking at truth tables for arguments, though. Consider the set of statements comprised of two statements related by each of the operators:

P	Q	P & Q	P ∨ Q	P → Q
T	T	T **T** T	T **T** T	T **T** T
T	F	T **F** F	T **T** F	T **F** F
F	T	F **F** T	F **T** T	F **T** T
F	F	F **F** F	F **T** F	F **T** F

One of the questions logicians ask about sets of sentences is whether it is possible for them *all to be true at the same time*. In terms of truth tables, this question is the question of whether there are any *rows* on the truth table on which all of the statements are true (since each row on the truth table represents one unique combination of truth values under which all of the statements are being considered). In the example above, there is such a row, the first row. Each of the statements is true on this row of the truth table.

If a set of statements has this characteristic; **there is at least one row (across) on their truth table on which they are all true**, we say the statements are *consistent*. Note that only one row is needed to show consistency. It makes no difference how many rows there on which the statements are all true, or how many rows there are on which they are *not* all true, or even if there are rows on which they are all *false*. The only issue here is whether there is *one* row on which they are all *true*.

Validity

The next (and final) issue for truth tables is the issue of validity. Recalling our definition of validity, an argument is valid if and only if it is *impossible* for the conclusion to be false WHILE the premises are true. This means that if we construct a truth table for an argument, and there is a single case (a single row accross) on the truth table on which the *conclusion is false* while the *premises are all true*, the argument is invalid. Only if there NO such case is the argument valid. Consider the following argument:

A & B
A → B
∴ A ∨ ~B

The symbol ∴ is the logical symbol for "therefore", and indicates the conclusion of the argument. The truth table for this argument would be constructed like the truth table for a set of statements:

A	B	A & B	A → B	∴A ∨ ~B
T	T	T **T** T	T **T** T	T **T** FT
T	F	T **F** F	T **F** F	T **T** TF
F	T	F **F** T	F **T** T	F **F** FT
F	F	F **F** F	F **T** F	F **F** TF

The question regarding this truth table is, again, whether there are ***ANY rows (across) on which the premises are TRUE and the conclusion is FALSE***. In this case, the answer is "NO." On the first row, the premises AND the conclusion are true. On the second row, both premises are false while the conclusion is true. On the third and fourth rows, although the conclusion is false, the first premise is false. So there are NO rows on which the premises are ALL true while the conclusion is false. So this argument is VALID.

Consider this argument:

A & (B ∨ C)
(A ∨ B) → C
∴ A → (B & C)

Since this argument has 3 terms, the truth table will have 8 lines:

A	B	C	A & (B ∨ C)	(A ∨ B) → C	∴A → (B & C)
T	T	T	T **T** T T T	T T T **T** T	T **T** T T T
T	T	F	T **T** T T F	T T T **F** F	T **F** T F F
T	F	T	T **T** F T T	T T F **T** T	T **F** F F T
T	F	F	T **F** F F F	T T F **F** F	T **F** F F F
F	T	T	F **F** T T T	F T T **T** T	F **T** T T T
F	T	F	F **F** T T F	F T T **F** F	F **T** T F F
F	F	T	F **F** F T F	F F F **T** T	F **T** F F T
F	F	F	F **F** F F F	F F F **T** F	F **T** F F F

The question is, *are there any rows on this truth table in which the premises are ALL true and the conclusion is false?* Remember, we are ONLY looking at the truth values under the main operators (in bold) and we are looking across the rows. There is such a row; the third row, which looks like this:

A	B	C	A & (B ∨ C)	(A ∨ B) → C	∴ A → (B & C)
T	F	T	T (T) F T T	T T F (T) T	T (F) F F T

On this row, when A is true, B is false, and C is true, both of the premises are true, and the conclusion is false. This shows that there is a case in which the premises are true and the conclusion is false, and this shows the argument to be INVALID. Remember, if there is ONE such row, that is all that is needed to show that an argument is invalid. In order for an argument to be valid, there must be NO rows on the truth table on which the premises are all true while the conclusion is false.

Exercises

Truth tables for consistency
Use a full truth table to test each of the following sets of statements for consistency. Be able to explain what indicates that the statements are consistent or inconsistent.

1. A & ~B	A ∨ B	A → ~B
2. A → (A ∨ B)	(A & ~B) → (A & B)	A & B
3. A ∨ (A ∨ B)	A & (A & ~B)	A → B
4. A ∨ (B → C)	(A & B) → ~C	B & ~C
5. B → (C & D)	~B & (C & D)	B ∨ (C ∨ D)

Truth tables for validity
Use a full table to test each of the following arguments for validity. Be able to explain what indicates that the argument is valid or invalid.

1. A & ~B	A ∨ B	∴ A → ~B
2. A → (A ∨ B)	(A & ~B) → (A & B)	∴ A & B
3. A ∨ (A ∨ B)	A & (A & ~B)	∴ A → B
4. A ∨ (B → C)	(A & B) → ~C	∴ B & ~C
5. B → (C & D)	~B & (C & D)	∴ B ∨ (C ∨ D)

3.10 – Shortened Truth Tables for Consistency and Validity

Since every added simple statement doubles the number of lines on a truth table, truth tables can become very large and unwieldy very quickly. In this section we will learn some methods for shortening the truth table method of analysis. Note, however, that with shortcuts come increased chances of making errors. The full truth table method, although it can be time-consuming, will always yield a correct answer with little chance of making mistakes.

The first shortcut method is a shortcut for filling out truth tables, even if a full truth table is to be constructed. For it, rather than making the columns of Ts and Fs on the left side of the table, and then transferring them over to the statements, it is quicker just to put the columns of Ts and Fs directly under the statements. The critical issue with this method is that *every* time a letter shows up in *any* statement it must get the *same* pattern of Ts and Fs under it, or else the truth table becomes invalid. In this example, the initial full truth table would look like this:

A & (B ∨ C)				(A ∨ B) → C				A → (B & C)		
T	T	T		T	T	T		T	T	T
T	T	F		T	T	F		T	T	F
T	F	T		T	F	T		T	F	T
T	F	F		T	F	F		T	F	F
F	T	T		F	T	T		F	T	T
F	T	F		F	T	F		F	T	F
F	F	T		F	F	T		F	F	T
F	F	F		F	F	F		F	F	F

Now, we have all of the truth value combinations under the letters, and we have written considerably fewer Ts and Fs! Note carefully that EVERY A in the statements has 4 Ts followed by 4 Fs, EVERY B has two Ts followed by 2 Fs, alternating, and EVERY C has one T followed by one F, alternating. Again, EVERY letter has to have exactly the same column EACH time it shows up in any statement, and wherever it shows up in the statement, whether it is the first or last letter, or somewhere in between.

Consistency

For shortened truth tables, it is important to start with an idea of what you're looking for. For consistency, we're looking for *a row on which all of the statements are TRUE (under the main operator)*. The next idea is "rows that are NOT the row we're looking for" (think of Star Wars, when Obi-Wan

Kenobi says to the Storm Troopers, "these aren't the droids you're looking for"). That is, as soon as we can determine that a row is NOT the row we're looking for, we can abandon it. When we're testing for consistency, if ANY statement in a row is FALSE, that row can NOT be the row we're looking for (we are look for a row on which ALL of the statements are true). So if we can spot cases in which statements will be false, we can rule out entire rows with little work.

In this example, we begin by filling in the truth table with the truth values of the simple statements (or negated simple statements):

A ∨ (B ∨ C)			(~A & ~B) → C			(B → C) & ~A		
T	T	T	FT	FT	T	T	T	FT
T	T	F	FT	FT	F	T	F	FT
T	F	T	FT	TF	T	F	T	FT
T	F	F	FT	TF	F	F	F	FT
F	T	T	TF	FT	T	T	T	TF
F	T	F	TF	FT	F	T	F	TF
F	F	T	TF	TF	T	F	T	TF
F	F	F	TF	TF	F	F	F	TF

We look for patterns in which statements will turn out to be false. This is where good knowledge of the basic truth tables is very valuable; it will help you see quickly when statements will be false. For instance, the conjunction on the far right will be false whenever ~A (the right conjunct) is false (whatever (B → C) is). ~A is false on the first 4 rows:

A ∨ (B ∨ C)			(~A & ~B) → C			(B → C) & ~A		
T	T	T	FT	FT	T	T	T	✗FT
T	T	F	FT	FT	F	T	F	✗FT
T	F	T	FT	TF	T	F	T	✗FT
T	F	F	FT	TF	F	F	F	✗FT
F	T	T	TF	FT	T	T	T	TF
F	T	F	TF	FT	F	T	F	TF
F	F	T	TF	TF	T	F	T	TF
F	F	F	TF	TF	F	F	F	TF

Similarly, if the left conjunct of a conjunction is false, the conjunction will be false, so whenever (B → C) is false, the third statement will also be false:

A ∨ (B ∨ C)	(~A & ~B) → C	(B → C) & ~A
T T T	FT FT T	T T ✗ FT
T T F	FT FT F	T F ✗ FT
T F T	FT TF T	F T ✗ FT
T F F	FT TF F	F F ✗ FT
F T T	TF FT T	T T TF
F T F	TF FT F	T F F ✗ TF
F F T	TF TF T	F T TF
F F F	TF TF F	F F TF

We have now eliminated 5 of the 8 rows without even looking at the first two statements! The first statement is a disjunction within a disjunction, so it will be false if all of the simple statements are false, which they are on row 8:

A ∨ (B ∨ C)	(~A & ~B) → C	(B → C) & ~A
T T T	FT FT T	T T ✗ FT
T T F	FT FT F	T F ✗ FT
T F T	FT TF T	F T ✗ FT
T F F	FT TF F	F F ✗ FT
F T T	TF FT T	T T TF
F T F	TF FT F	T F F ✗ TF
F F T	TF TF T	F T TF
F ✗ F FF	TF TF F	F F TF

Now, the only rows we have left to examine more closely are rows 5 and 7. Working out the truth values on row 5, we get:

A ∨ (B ∨ C)	(~A & ~B) → C	(B → C) & ~A
T T T	FT FT T	T T ✗ FT
T T F	FT FT F	T F ✗ FT
T F T	FT TF T	F T ✗ FT
T F F	FT TF F	F F ✗ FT
F (T) T T T	TF F FT (T) T	T T T (T) TF
F T F	TF FT F	T F F ✗ TF
F F T	TF TF T	F T TF
F ✗ F FF	TF TF F	F F TF

On this row, ALL of the statements come out to be true. This is the row we were looking for. It means that our set of statements is consistent (remember, ONE row on which all of the statements are true is all that we need to show consistency – we haven't even looked at row 7, but that doesn't matter, because we have already found one row).

The basic rules for the shortcut method of testing for consistency are:

1. Begin with the simplest statement or a statement that will quickly yield Fs.
2. Abandon any row on which *any statement is FALSE* (place an X on the F under the main operator of these rows, cross the row out, etc.).
3. As soon as you have a single row on which all the statements are TRUE, you can declare the statements CONSISTENT.
4. If, after examining ALL rows, you have NO rows on which all the statements are TRUE, you can declare the statements INCONSISTENT.

Validity

For arguments, the row we're looking for is *a row in which the premises are all TRUE and the conclusion is FALSE*. That means that any row on which the conclusion is TRUE is *not* the row we're looking for. So it is quicker to start by determining the truth value of the conclusion on EACH row before even looking at the premises. In this example, we get this result:

A & (B ∨ C)			(A ∨ B) → C			∴ A → (B & C)				
T	T	T	T	T	T	T	**T**	T	T	T
T	T	F	T	T	F	T	**F**	T	F	F
T	F	T	T	F	T	T	**F**	F	F	T
T	F	F	T	F	F	T	**F**	F	F	F
F	T	T	F	T	T	F	**T**	T	T	T
F	T	F	F	T	F	F	**T**	T	F	F
F	F	T	F	F	T	F	**T**	F	F	T
F	F	F	F	F	F	F	**T**	F	F	F

We can look at the truth table for the conclusion and rule out all of the rows that are NOT the row we're looking for. We're looking for a row with a FALSE conclusion. Here, the conclusion is true on all but three of the rows (it is true on rows 1, 5, 6, 7, and 8, and it is false on rows 2, 3, and 4). We can put an X through the T (or cross off the row) on all of the rows on which the conclusion is true. It is also helpful to circle the Fs, showing that these are rows we have to pay attention to.

A Formal Introduction to Critical Thinking

A & (B ∨ C)	(A ∨ B) → C	∴ A → (B & C)
T T T	T T T	T ✗ T T T
T T F	T T F	T Ⓕ T F F
T F T	T F T	T Ⓕ F F T
T F F	T F F	T Ⓕ F F F
F T T	F T T	F ✗ T T T
F T F	F T F	F ✗ T F F
F F T	F F T	F ✗ F F T
F F F	F F F	F ✗ F F F

Now, we only have to work out the truth values of the *premises* on three rows (since they are the only ones that can be the row we're looking for. So we've already shortened our work considerably.

When we look at the premises on these three rows we can think this: if we come across a premise that is FALSE, it is not the row we're looking for, because we're looking for a row on which the premises are all TRUE and the conclusion is false.

On rows 2 and 4, the second premise is false, so we can abandon those rows.

A & (B ∨ C)	(A ∨ B) → C	∴ A → (B & C)
T T T	T T T	T ✗ T T T
T T F	T T T ✗ F	T Ⓕ T F F
T F T	T F T	T Ⓕ F F T
T F F	T T F ✗ F	T Ⓕ F F F
F T T	F T T	F ✗ T T T
F T F	F T F	F ✗ T F F
F F T	F F T	F ✗ F F T
F F F	F F F	F ✗ F F F

The only row left to check now is row 3.

A & (B ∨ C)	(A ∨ B) → C	∴ A → (B & C)
T T T	T T T	T ✗ T T T
T T F	T T T ✗ F	T Ⓕ T F F
T Ⓣ F T T	T T F Ⓣ T	T Ⓕ F F T
T F F	T T F ✗ F	T Ⓕ F F F
F T T	F T T	F ✗ T T T
F T F	F T F	F ✗ T F F
F F T	F F T	F ✗ F F T
F F F	F F F	F ✗ F F F

This turns out to be the row we're looking for – all of the premises are true and the conclusion is false. This means that the argument is INVALID (remember, finding the row we're looking for is bad for arguments, but good for consistency). But we determined this with much less work than before.

The general rules for this shortcut for validity are:

1. Begin by determining the truth values of the conclusion.
2. Any row on which the *conclusion is TRUE* can be abandoned.
3. For the rows on which the conclusion is FALSE, begin determining the truth values of the premises.
4. Abandon any row on which any *premise is FALSE*.
5. As soon as you have a single row on which the premises are TRUE and the conclusion is FALSE, you can declare the argument INVALID.
6. If, after examining ALL rows, there are NO rows on which the premises are TRUE and the conclusion is FALSE you can declare the argument VALID.

A Formal Introduction to Critical Thinking

Exercises

Truth tables for consistency
Use a shortened truth table to test each of the following sets of statements for consistency. Be able to explain what indicates that the statements are consistent or inconsistent.

1. A ∨ (B → C)   (A & B) → ~C   B & ~C
2. B → (C & D)   ~B & (C → D)   B ∨ (C ∨ D)
3. A & (B & ~C)   B ∨ (~A ∨ ~C)   (C → A) & ~B
4. (B & A) → (A → ~C)   (A ∨ B) → C   (B & C) → (A & B)
5. (A ∨ B) → (B → ~C)   ((A & B) → ~C) → B   (A & B) & ~C

Truth tables for validity
Use shortened truth tables to test these arguments for validity.

1. A ∨ (B → C)   (A & B) → ~C   ∴ B & ~C
2. B → (C & D)   ~B & (C → D)   ∴ B ∨ (C ∨ D)
3. A & (B & ~C)   B ∨ (~A ∨ ~C)   ∴ (C → A) & ~B
4. (B & A) → (A → ~C)   (A ∨ B) → C   ∴ (B & C)→(A & B)
5. (A ∨ B) → (B → ~C)   ((A & B) → ~C) → B   ∴(A & B) & ~C

3.11 – The Indirect Method for Consistency and Validity

Consistency

The shortcut methods we have just learned will shorten the process of constructing truth tables considerably. But they are still limited. What if you have an argument that has 5 simple statements? The truth table will have $2^5 = 32$ lines! Even the shortcut method will be cumbersome and slow for that. But there is an even shorter method.

Knowing the characteristic truth tables of the operators (it is vital that you know them by heart by this time), it is possible to limit the number of rows that have to be considered to only a few, even when the number of simple statements is large. Consider the following set of statements, and the question of consistency:

(A & B) & C   (D ∨ E) → ~B   F → (E & A)   F ∨ C

There are 5 simple statements in this set, so it would require a truth table of 32 lines. However, we know what row we are looking for. We are looking for *a row on which all of the statements are true*. We can try to *construct* such a row for these statements. If we are able to, we will know that the set is consistent; if not, we will know it is not consistent. To begin constructing a test-row, we place a T in a circle under each of the main operators of the set of statements, symbolizing what we want to show:

(A & B) & C   (D ∨ E) → ~B   F → (E & A)   F ∨ C
     Ⓣ   Ⓣ   Ⓣ   Ⓣ

Next, we consider the main operators of each of the statements. They are, from left to right; &, →, →, and ∨. Now we think about the characteristic truth tables of these operators. We ask, are there any operators that can be true in only a limited number of cases? The → is true in 3 of four rows of its truth table, the ∨ is true on 3 of four rows, but the & is only true on one of its four rows (the case in which the left and right conjuncts are both true). So, we know that the first statement, in order to be true, must be true on both sides of the operator. That is, (A & B) must be true, and C must be true. We can fill these truth values in under the operators:

(A & B) & C   (D ∨ E) → ~B   F → (E & A)   F ∨ C
  T   ⓉT   Ⓣ   Ⓣ   Ⓣ

Now, (A & B) is another conjunction. That means that, again, both of its conjuncts (A and B) must be true in order for it to be true. So the first statement, if true, must look like this:

(A & B) & C   (D ∨ E) → ~B   F → (E & A)   F ∨ C
T T T (T)T   (T)   (T)   (T)

Now we know that some of the simple statements MUST have certain truth values, because if they don't have these values, the first statement will be false, but we have to make ALL of the statements true. We can now take this information and use it to determine the truth values of other statements, because a simple statement must have the same truth value throughout the statements on a particular row of a truth table. Moving on to the second statement, since we already know that B must be true, we can place a "T" under the B, and it follows that ~B must be false:

(A & B) & C   (D ∨ E) → ~B   F → (E & A)   F ∨ C
T T T (T)T   (T) FT   (T)   (T)

The second statement is a conditional. A conditional statement with a false consequent (right side) will only be true if it also has a false antecedent (because T → F = F, but F → F = T). Since ~B is false, in order to make that statement true, (D ∨ E) must be false. But D and E must both be false for (D ∨ E) to be false. So we can complete the truth values for the second statement:

(A & B) & C   (D ∨ E) → ~B   F → (E & A)   F ∨ C
T T T (T)T   F F F(T) FT   (T)   (T)

We now have two true statements, and more information. A is true (from the first statement) and E is false (from the second statement), so (E & A) in the third statement will be false:

(A & B) & C   (D ∨ E) → ~B   F → (E & A)   F ∨ C
T T T (T)T   F F F(T) FT   (T) T F F   (T)

The third statement is a conditional; since it is false on the right side, it will only be true if the F (on the left side) is false (remember we *want* to make it true). So we can make that statement true by making F false.

(A & B) & C   (D ∨ E) → ~B   F → (E & A)   F ∨ C
T T T (T)T   F F F(T) FT   F(T) T F F   (T)

In the last statement, we already know that C is true, and F is False, so the disjunction will be true:

(A & B) & C	(D ∨ E) → ~B	F → (E & A)	F ∨ C
T T T ⓉT	F F F Ⓣ FT	F Ⓣ T F F	FⓉ T

Consider what we have done. We have constructed a set of truth values that will make ALL of the statements true. We can now answer the question; is it possible for all of these statements to be true at the same time? The answer is "yes," even though we have considered only one row. But, remember, for consistency, *one* row on which all of the statements are true at the same time is all we need.

Now use the same operation to test this set.

(A & B) & ~C   (D ∨ E) → ~B   (E ∨ F) → C   F ∨ C

We begin the test in the same way, placing circled Ts under each main operator.

(A & B) & ~C   (D ∨ E) → ~B   (E ∨ F) → C   F ∨ C
     Ⓣ   Ⓣ   Ⓣ   Ⓣ

The first statement, again, is a conjunction within a conjunction. It will only be true if (A & B) is true and ~C is true. For (A & B) to be true, A and B must both be true. For ~C to be true, C must be false:

(A & B) & ~C   (D ∨ E) → ~B   (E ∨ F) → C   F ∨ C
T T T Ⓣ TF   Ⓣ   Ⓣ   Ⓣ

We take the information from the first statement and make the second statement true. B is true, ~B is false. That means that the left side of the conditional must be false for the conditional to be true, which means that D and E both have to be false.

(A & B) & ~C   (D ∨ E) → ~B   (E ∨ F) → C   F ∨ C
T T T Ⓣ TF   F F F Ⓣ FT   Ⓣ   Ⓣ

We know C is false (from statement 1), so we can put it into the last statement (The order that you fill in the statements makes no difference):

(A & B) & ~C   (D ∨ E) → ~B   (E ∨ F) → C   F ∨ C
T T T Ⓣ TF   F F F Ⓣ FT   Ⓣ   Ⓣ F

To make that disjunction true, we have to make F true:

(A & B) & ~C	(D ∨ E) → ~B	(E ∨ F) → C	F ∨ C
T T T (T) TF	F F F (T)FT	(T)	T(T)F

Now, the F in the third statement must be true (from the fourth statement), and the E in the third statement must be false (from the second statement), which makes the disjunction (E ∨ F) true:

(A & B) & ~C	(D ∨ E) → ~B	(E ∨ F) → C	F ∨ C
T T T (T) TF	F F F (T)FT	F T T (T)	T(T)F

Now we have a problem. E is false, from statement two; F is true, from statement four; and C is false, from statement one. If we plug in those values in statement three, it makes it false! And, it turns out (you can try this if you want), if we change any of the truth values to make the third statement true, we would have to change the corresponding truth value for that or those letters in other statements, and it would make one of the other statements false! We signify this by placing an X over the T in the third statement, which means that we were unable to make this statement true along with all of the others.

(A & B) & ~C	(D ∨ E) → ~B	(E ∨ F) → C	F ∨ C
T T T (T)TF	F F F (T)FT	F T T ⊗	T(T)F

If C is true, the first statement will be false, but if C is false, the third statement will be false. If E is false, the third statement is false, but if E it true, the second statement will be false. If F is true, the third statement will be false, but if F is false, the fourth statement will be false.

An important question now arises. Can we conclude anything? We've only looked at one row on our truth table. But, since there is ONLY ONE combination of truth values that will make the *first* statement true (the combination we have in this row), we can say definitively at this point that it is NOT possible to make all of these statements true at the same time (because making the first statement true makes the third statement false, and making the third statement true would always make another statement false. This set of statements, then, is *inconsistent*. It is impossible to make them all true at the same time.

Sometimes each statement can be made true in more than one way. In this case, you have to examine a row for the *least* number of ways to make any of the statements true. For instance:

(A & B) ∨ C   (C & B) → ~A

There are three ways to make a disjunction true and three ways to make a conditional true. We should use the method with the *fewest* possibilities. Since both statements have the same number, we just pick one. We will make three rows of Ts under the main operators.

Next, we fill in all the ways that the disjunction can be true. From the truth table, the set of truth values under which a disjunction are true are T-T; T-F; F-T (the disjunction is false on the F-F row). The two statements in this disjunction are (A & B) and C. We put the Ts and Fs under each of those statements:

```
(A & B) ∨ C          (A & B) → ~C
   T   (T)T               (T)
   T   (T)F               (T)
   F   (T)T               (T)
```

We can work out each row independently. For the first row, if (A & B) is going to be true, both A and B have to be true:

```
(A & B) ∨ C          (A & B) → ~C
T T T (T)T               (T)
   T  (T)F               (T)
   F  (T)T               (T)
```

We can fill those truth values in for the second statement:

```
(A & B) ∨ C          (A & B) → ~C
T T T (T)T           T T T (X)FT
   T  (T)F               (T)
   F  (T)T               (T)
```

This assignment makes the second statement false, so we place an X over the T and we know that the first row is NOT the row we're looking for. Can we say the set is inconsistent? Not yet. There are other ways that the first statement can be made true, so there are other possibilities to consider. Now we will move to the second possibility, on the second row. In it, C is

A Formal Introduction to Critical Thinking

false, and (A & B) is true.   A and B individually must be true, so we can complete the row:

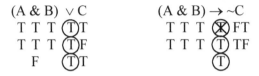

   On this row, both statements come out true. We have a truth-value assignment on which BOTH of the statements are true. This shows the statements to be *consistent*. The fact that they can't both be made true on the first assignment means nothing. For consistency, all we need is a *single* row on the truth table on which all of the statements are true. Similarly, the fact that we haven't looked at the third possibility means nothing. Again, all we need is a single row on the truth on which all of the statements are true. As soon as such a row is found, we are finished. On the other hand, IF we had completed ALL of the rows and NONE of them was a case in which ALL of the statements were true, then we would have shown the statements to be *inconsistent*.

The indirect method for consistency

1. Find the statement in the set that can be made true in the fewest number of ways (there will often be more than one way).
2. Make that statement true in ALL the ways it can be made true.
3. Use those truth values on each row to try to make the rest of the statements true.
4. You are finished when:
  i) You create a row on which all of the statements are true – the set is CONSISTENT, OR
  ii) You examine all the rows you have and NONE of them are a row on which all of the statements are true – the set is INCONSISTENT.

Validity

   The indirect test for validity is the same basic operation as the indirect test for consistency, other than the difference in what is being tested for. For validity, the row we're looking for is *a row on which the premises are all true while the conclusion is false*. So, consider this argument:

  A → (D & F) (D → ~B) ∨ ~H H ∨ J   ∴ (A & B) → C

We begin by setting up the condition we're looking for; in this case, true premises and a false conclusion:

A → (D & F)   (D → ~B) ∨ ~H   H ∨ J   ∴ (A & B) → C
Ⓣ   Ⓣ   Ⓣ   Ⓕ

Now we begin the process of examining possibilities. Since the premises must be true and the conclusion false, we have two places to look. In this case, the conclusion can be false in only one way, while all of the premises can be true in more than one way. The quickest way to test the argument is by starting with the conclusion. A conditional is false only in the case where the antecedent (left side) is true and the consequent (right side) is false:

A → (D & F)   (D → ~B) ∨ ~H   H ∨ J   ∴ (A & B) → C
Ⓣ   Ⓣ   Ⓣ   T T T Ⓕ F

We can now put the value for A in the first statement:

A → (D & F)   (D → ~B) ∨ ~H   H ∨ J   ∴ (A & B) → C
TⓉ   Ⓣ   Ⓣ   T T T Ⓕ F

Since the first statement is a conditional, with a true antecedent, it must have a true consequent (we want to make the *premises true*), so D and F both have to be true:

A → (D & F)   (D → ~B) ∨ ~H   H ∨ J   ∴ (A & B) → C
TⓉ T T T   Ⓣ   Ⓣ   T T T Ⓕ F

We can place the values for D (from the first statement) and B (from the fourth statement) in the second statement. This makes (D → ~B) false.

A → (D & F)   (D → ~B) ∨ ~H   H ∨ J   ∴ (A & B) → C
TⓉ T T T   T F FT Ⓣ   Ⓣ   T T T Ⓕ F

(D → ~B) is false, so to make the disjunction true, ~H will have to be true and H false:

A → (D & F)   (D → ~B) ∨ ~H   H ∨ J   ∴ (A & B) → C
TⓉ T T T   T F FTⓉTF   Ⓣ   T T T Ⓕ F

A Formal Introduction to Critical Thinking

Since H is false, to make (H ∨ J) true, J will have to be true. Since J has not been assigned a truth value anywhere else, it can be made true:

A → (D & F)	(D → ~B) ∨ ~H	H ∨ J	∴ (A & B) → C
T (T) T T T	T F FT (T) TF	F (T) T	T T T (F) F

Now, consider this row. We have constructed a situation or a row in which the premises of the argument are true and the conclusion is false. Note again that it doesn't matter if there are any other such cases, nor how many there are. A single truth value assignment in which the premises are true and the conclusion is false is enough to prove an argument *invalid*. We found (by creating) the row we were looking for, so the argument is invalid.

Now, consider this slightly-revised argument:

A → (D & F)	(D → ~B) ∨ ~H	H ∨ C	∴ (A & B) → C
(T)	(T)	(T)	(F)

Again, we want to make the conclusion false, which can be done in only one way:

A → (D & F)	(D → ~B) ∨ ~H	H ∨ C	∴ (A & B) → C
(T)	(T)	(T)	T T T (F) F

We can now put the value for A in the first statement:

A → (D & F)	(D → ~B) ∨ ~H	H ∨ C	∴ (A & B) → C
T (T)	(T)	(T)	T T T (F) F

Since the first statement is a conditional, with a true antecedent, it must have a true consequent (we want to make the *premises true*), so D and F both have to be true:

A → (D & F)	(D → ~B) ∨ ~H	H ∨ C	∴ (A & B) → C
T (T) T T T	(T)	(T)	T T T (F) F

We can place the values for D (from the first statement) and B (from the fourth statement) in the second statement. This makes (D → ~B) false.

A → (D & F)	(D → ~B) ∨ ~H	H ∨ C	∴ (A & B) → C
T (T) T T T	T F FT (T)	(T)	T T T (F) F

(D → ~B) is false, so to make the disjunction true, ~H will have to be true and H false:

A → (D & F)   (D → ~B) ∨ ~H   H ∨ C   ∴ (A & B) → C
T Ⓣ TTT   T F FTⓉTF   Ⓣ   TT T ⒻF

Now consider (H ∨ C), the remaining premise. We know C is false, from the conclusion. We know H is false, from the second statement. So (H ∨ C) must be false. We signify this by drawing an X through the hypothetical T under the ∨, showing that it failed to be possible to make it true.

A → (D & F)   (D → ~B) ∨ ~H   H ∨ C   ∴ (A & B) → C
T Ⓣ TTT   T F FTⓉTF   FⓧF   TT T ⒻF

This means that on the *only* truth value assignment on which the conclusion is false, one of the premises is also false. We can assert that there are NO cases in which the premises are all true while the conclusion is false, so the argument is *valid*.

As with testing sets of statements for consistency, if none of the statements have only one truth value assignment on which it is true (for the premises) or false (for the conclusion), you must examine *all* of the possibilities for the statement with the least number of ways it can be made true or false.

(A ∨ B) → (A & C)   ~C ∨ B   ∴ A & B

This conclusion, a conjunction, can be made false in one of three ways; if A is true and B false, if A is false and B true, or if both are false. So we have to examine each of these possibilities:

(A ∨ B) → (A & C)   ~C ∨ B   ∴ A & B
        Ⓣ   Ⓣ   T Ⓕ F
        Ⓣ   Ⓣ   F Ⓕ T
        Ⓣ   Ⓣ   F Ⓕ F

Taking the first row first, the values for A and B can be filled in in the first statement:

A Formal Introduction to Critical Thinking

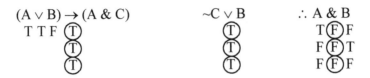

The disjunction, (A ∨ B), will be true. To make the conditional true, the consequent (A & C) must be true. We know A is true; C must also be true:

Since C is true, ~C will be false. Since B is false, the disjunction (~C ∨ B) will be false, so we can't make the second premise true.

Since the premises on this row are not all true, it is NOT the row we're looking for. Can we stop? No. Like with consistency, we cannot stop until we either find the row we're looking for OR examine all the possibilities. So we have to continue to the second line. Here we know that A is false and B is true. The disjunction in the first premise will again be true, but since A is false, it will make the conjunction in that premise false, which will make the conditional false.

$$(A \vee B) \rightarrow (A \& C) \qquad \sim C \vee B \qquad \therefore A \& B$$

At this point, we haven't figured out what the second premise is, or what C is, but it doesn't matter, because the values for A and B render the first premise false. The second row is NOT the row we're looking for, but

---

[8] A question mark on a truth table means that we don't know what the truth value of this statement is, and it doesn't matter. Since A is false, the conjunction (A & C) will be false, whatever value C has. A question mark is the symbol to use here, to indicate that we don't know or care what C is.

we have one more row to consider. We have to go on to the last row. Since A and B are both false, the antecedent of the first conditional will be false. That means that the conditional will be true even though the consequent is also false, because A is false. We don't know what C is, so we will leave it blank here in case we determine its value later.

(A ∨ B) → (A & C)	~C ∨ B	∴ A & B
T T F Ⓣ T T T	F T Ⓧ F	T Ⓕ F
F T T Ⓧ F F ?	Ⓣ	F Ⓕ T
F F F Ⓣ F F	Ⓣ	F Ⓕ F

In the second premise, B is false, so ~C must be true (we're trying to make the premises true, remember). Since C hasn't been determined anywhere, it can be made false, which will make ~C true, and will make the disjunction true. Notice that we went back to the first premise and filled in the value for C there; this is important, to show that all truth values have been assigned – it doesn't change anything in the first premise.

(A ∨ B) → (A & C)	~C ∨ B	∴ A & B
T T F Ⓣ T T T	F T Ⓧ F	T Ⓕ F
F T T Ⓧ F F ?	Ⓣ	F Ⓕ T
F F F Ⓣ F F F	T F Ⓣ F	F Ⓕ F

In this case again, we have found the row we were looking for; true premises with a false conclusion. The argument is INVALID. One such row is all we need. If we had NOT found any rows with true premises and a false conclusion, we would have shown the argument to be valid.

The indirect method for validity

1. Make the conclusion FALSE in ALL the ways it can be made false (there may be more than one way).
2. Use those truth values in the premises to try to make the premises true.
3. You are finished when:
   i) You create a row on which the conclusion is false and the premises are true – the argument is INVALID, OR
   ii) You examine all the rows you have and NONE of them are a row on which the conclusion is false while the premises are true – the argument is VALID.

A Formal Introduction to Critical Thinking

Exercises

Truth tables for consistency
Use an indirect truth table to test each of the following sets of statements for consistency. Be able to explain what indicates that the statements are consistent or inconsistent.

1.   A & (B & ~C)   B ∨ (~A ∨ ~C)   (C → A) & ~B
2.   (A ∨ B) → (B → ~C)   ((A & B) → C) → ~B   (A & B) & ~C
3.   (B & A) → (A → C)   ~[(A & B) → C]   (B & C) → (A & B)
4.   A → B   (B → C) & ~(A ∨ E)   D & (E ∨ B)   A → E
5.   A → B   (A & C) & (B → ~D)   ~D → C   D ∨ ~C

Truth tables for validity
Use the indirect method to test these arguments for validity.

1.   (B & A) → (A → ~C)   (A ∨ B) → ~C   ∴ (B & C) → (A → ~B)
2.   (A ∨ B) → (B → ~C)   ((A & B) → C) → B   ∴(B → A) ∨ ~C
3.   (A & C) → B   ~C → D   (D & B) ∨ C   A → D ∴ A &B
4.   C → A   D → A   E → A   (A ∨ ~C) → B   D ∨ E   ∴ A & B
5.   B ∨ C
     C → (D & ~E)
     (D → E) ∨ (A & G)
     G & H
     (H & D) → C   ∴ A & B

Chapter 4: The Natural System of Deduction

4.1 – Introduction

The system we will learn in this chapter is referred to as the *Natural System of Deduction* (ND). In it we will be doing problems that are called "deductions" or "derivations" or "proofs." A derivation, as I will call them, is a set of steps in which you begin with some given information and some rules, and you *derive* some information from the initial set using the rules. Truth tables are essentially a derivation; you start with some statements, you put Ts and Fs on the table according to the rules, and you end up with (derive) an answer to the question. In this section we will learn a different approach. Our interest in this section is only in testing arguments for validity. We will start with the general principle, ***if you can derive the conclusion of the argument from the premises using the rules, the argument is valid***.

The rules of ND are divided into two categories; rules of inference and rules of replacement. We will begin with the rules of inference. The rules of ND are rules that claim that, if you know certain statements are true, you can *deduce* or *derive* the truth of other statements from them.

4.2 – The Rules of Inference
Conjunction Elimination (&E)[9]

The rules will be presented according to the pattern, *if you know this, you would also know (or, you can derive, or therefore,) this*.
For instance,

If you know $\underline{p \ \& \ q}$[10]
You would also know (therefore) $\therefore \ p$

That is, if you know that a *conjunction* of two statements, p & q, is *true*, then you would know that p is true, because both statements in a conjunction must be true for the conjunction to be true. By the same reasoning,

---

[9] This rule is sometimes referred to as "Simplification (Simp)."
[10] As with truth table, lower-case letters are *variables* – they can stand for ANY statement, simple or compound.

If you know   p & q
You would also know (therefore)   ∴ q

That is, if you know that a conjunction of two statements, p & q, is true, then you would know that q is true, because both statements in a conjunction must be true for the conjunction to be true.

Disjunctive Syllogism (DS)

Many of the rules of ND are in fact mini-arguments (this is why they are called rules of *inference*). They follow from a general rule that says that any argument form that can be shown to be valid may be introduced as a rule in the system. This rule is based on the fact that if an argument form is valid, any argument that is an example of that form will be a valid argument. Furthermore, if the premises of a valid argument are true, then the conclusion is guaranteed to be true. So, if the premises of a valid argument form are given in a derivation, the conclusion of that argument form will be guaranteed to be true, so the form, including the conclusion may be introduced as a rule of derivation. *Disjunctive Syllogism* is the first of this sort of rule to be introduced. The rule is:

If you know   or
                                          p ∨ q
AND you know   not ~p
You would also know (therefore)   ∴ q   thun if it's q

That is, if the *disjunction* p ∨ q is *true* and p is *false* (~p is true), then q must be true. In other words, if p OR q is true, and p is NOT true, then q must be true.

Consider this as an argument (a *syllogism* is an argument with just 2 premises) with p ∨ q and ~p as the premises and q as the conclusion. Now consider an indirect truth table test of the argument:

p ∨ q   ~p   / q
T (T) F   (X) T   (F)

This argument is valid. That is, if q (the conclusion) is false, then to make p ∨ q true, p must be true. But if p is true, ~p is false, so the premises cannot be made true.

You can derive p as well if you have the disjunction and the negation of q:

If you know	p ∨ q
AND you know	~q
You would also know (therefore)	∴ p

If p OR q is true, and q is NOT true, then p must be true.

4.3 – Introduction to Derivations

ND is a system of *derivations*. A derivation is a process by which certain statements are *given* as true, and then other statements are *derived* from the initial set according to the rules. So far we have only two rules, but they are enough to begin doing derivations.

In a derivation, certain statements are given as true. For instance:

1. A ∨ B   Given
2. ~A   Given

"Given" in these statements means "given as true" or "For this problem, take these statements to be true." The point of the derivation is to start with what you are given and use the rules to *derive* other statements. In this case, the two lines given are an instance of Disjunctive Syllogism. DS tells us what can be deduced or derived from these statements. Intuitively, statement 1 says that A OR B is true, and statement 2 says that ~A is true (or A is false). So we can deduce that B must be true. We would write this as:

1. A ∨ B   Given
2. ~A   Given
3. B   1,2 DS

Notice, at the right side of line 3, it says "1,2 DS." This is called a *justification. Every line of a derivation must have a justification.* A justification contains two pieces of information;

1. the line or lines that the new statement is derived from and
2. the rule that was used to derive it.

In the case, we would read line 3 as, "we derived a B on line 3, using lines 1 and 2 and the rule DS (Disjunctive syllogism). Again, *every line of a derivation must have a justification.*

Now consider this beginning of a derivation:

1. A & ~B   Given
2. B ∨ C   Given

Again, we want to see if and how we can apply the rules we know to deduce or derive statements from the statements given. In this case, the first statement is a conjunction. Conjunction elimination says that if a conjunction is true, we can derive either (or both) of the conjuncts individually. So, we can write, as line 3:

1. A & ~B   Given
2. B ∨ C   Given
3. A   1 &E

This says, "we can derive A from line 1, using Conjunction Elimination (&E)." We can also derive the ~B from line 1, using Conjunction Elimination:

1. A & ~B   Given
2. B ∨ C   Given
3. A   1 &E
4. ~B   1 &E

Now we ask, "what more can we do?" The general strategy of derivations is to take information that you have derived (remember, all derived lines, if derived properly, are guaranteed to be true) and use it with other information you have to derive more information. Derivations can use *any* previous line, whether it was given or derived. Also, lines don't have to be next to each other or in the order that the rule is given to be used. Notice that line 2 (given) is "B ∨ C" and line 4 is "~B" (derived). That means that we can apply the rule of Disjunctive Syllogism to lines 2 and 4, and derive a C:

1. A & ~B   Given
2. B ∨ C   Given
3. A   1 &E
4. ~B   1 &E
5. C   2,4 DS

Line 5 reads, "we derive a C from lines 2 and 4 using the rule DS." We have now derived all that can be derived from these statements, so there is no more to be done.

The point of derivations is to evaluate arguments. The rule, remember, is, if the conclusion of an argument can be derived from the premises, the argument is valid. Suppose the two statements in the last example were provided as the premises of an argument, with C as the conclusion:

A & ~B
B ∨ C
Therefore, C

We would have *proven the argument valid* in the derivation, because we derived the conclusion from the premises. This is what we will be doing with derivations.

Consider this argument:

1.	A ∨ ~B	Given	
2.	B ∨ C	Given	
3.	~A	Given	/∴ C

In this case, the three premises are presented as lines with line numbers, and the conclusion (C) is set to the right (∴ is the symbol for "therefore"). The conclusion is what we are trying to derive – this is our goal. As before, we begin by isolating statements that we can apply the rules to. In this case, we can apply the rule of Disjunctive Syllogism to lines 1 and 3, and derive a ~B:

1.	A ∨ ~B	Given	
2.	B ∨ C	Given	
3.	~A	Given	/∴ C
4.	~B	1,3 DS	

Keeping track of tildes can become tricky in derivations. We derived ~B on line 4, not B. That's because line 1 says that A is true or ~B is true (not B is true). Since A is not true, we have to derive the other disjunct, as it was written in the disjunction. In this case the other disjunct has a tilde on it, so it must keep the tilde. Now, we can apply DS to lines 2 and 4, to derive a C:

1. A ∨ ~B   Given
2. B ∨ C   Given
3. <u>~A</u>   <u>Given   /∴ C</u>
4. ~B   1,3 DS
5. C   2,4 DS

Once the conclusion has been derived, the proof is over.

Deriving Compound Statements

Look at this argument:

1. A ∨ (B & ~C)   Given
2. ~A   Given
3. <u>C ∨ D</u>   <u>Given   /∴ D</u>

Line 1 is a disjunction. It has A as one disjunct and (B & ~C) as another disjunct. So we know that either A is true or (B & ~C) is true. Line 2 asserts ~A, or that A is false. Since A is false, the other side of the disjunction must be true. So, the whole compound statement, (B & ~C) must be true. We write this as;

1. A ∨ (B & ~C)   Given
2. ~A   Given
3. <u>C ∨ D</u>   <u>Given   /∴ D</u>
4. B & ~C   1,2 DS

The justification is normal; we derived B & ~C from lines 1 and 2 using DS. Once you have this compound statement, it can be used for further derivations. Here's how this problem would end up:

1. A ∨ (B & ~C)   Given
2. ~A   Given
3. <u>C ∨ D</u>   <u>Given   /∴ D</u>
4. B & ~C   1,2 DS
5. ~C   4 &E
6. D   3,5 DS

Exercises

Try the following exercises involving just &E and DS:

A. 1. A ∨ (C ∨ D)   Given
   2. ~A & ~C   Given   /∴ D

B. 1. ~A & ~B   Given
   2. A ∨ ~D   Given
   3. B ∨ (D ∨ ~E)   Given   /∴ ~E

C. 1. P ∨ ((Q & ~R) ∨ S) Given
   2. ~S & ~P   Given
   3. R ∨ T   Given   /∴ T

D. 1. (D ∨ E) & (F ∨ G)   Given
   2. H ∨ (~D & ~G)   Given
   3. ~H   Given   /∴ E AND F

E. 1. (~A & ~B) & (B ∨ (C ∨ A))   Given   /∴C

F. 1. [(H ∨ ~I) & (H ∨ ~J)] & (~H & ~K) Given
   2. K ∨ [(I ∨ ~L) & (J ∨ ~M)]   Given
   3. L ∨ N   Given
   4. M ∨ O   Given /∴ N AND O

G. 1. (M & N) ∨ (~P & ~Q) Given
   2. ~(M & N)   Given
   3. (P ∨ R) & (Q ∨ S)   Given   /∴R AND S

4.4 – More Derivation Rules

Conjunction Introduction (&I)

If you know	p
And you know	q_____
You would also know (therefore)	∴ p & q

This is a construction or introduction rule. It tells us that if we know that two statements are true, we can derive the truth of the conjunction of the two statements. This is because if two statements are true, the conjunction of the two statements is necessarily true as well.

Modus Ponens (MP)

There are two rules in ND based on conditionals. These are the two most common and most-used rules in logic, so you must know them well. The first is Modus Ponens (these rules were identified by Latin logicians and so have Latin names):

If you know	p → q
And you know	p_____
You would also know (therefore)	∴ q

If you know that *if* p is true, then q is true, and you know that p *is* true, it follows that q is true. For instance, if it is true that IF it is raining, then I carry my umbrella, and it is true that it is raining, then it would *have* to be true that I would be carrying my umbrella. This can be demonstrated using an indirect truth table proof:

$$\frac{p \rightarrow q}{F\textcircled{T}F} \quad \frac{p}{\textcircled{X}} \quad \frac{/q}{\textcircled{F}}$$

If q (the conclusion) is false, then p → q will be true only if p is false. But if p is false, then the premise that is just p cannot be true. So the argument and the rule based on it are valid.

Modus Tollens (MT)

Modus Tollens is the counter-part to Modus Ponens. It is very common and quite tricky. It asserts this:

If you know	p → q
And you know	~q
You would also know (therefore)	∴~p

If p → q is true and q (the consequent) is false, then p must also be false (otherwise p → q will be false). Again if it is true that IF it is raining, then I carry my umbrella, and I DO NOT (it is false that I) have my umbrella, then it would have to be NOT (false that it is) raining. On an indirect truth table:

p → q   ~q   / ~p
T Ⓣ T   Ⓧ T   Ⓕ T

If ~p (the conclusion) is false, then p is true. To make p → q true, q must be true. But if q is true, then the premise ~q must be false. So the argument and the rule based on it are valid.

Two Common Conditional Derivation Errors

Modus Ponens and Modus Tollens are often confused with the following two INVALID argument or rule forms:

Denying the Antecedent

If you know	p → q
And you know	~p
Would you also know?	∴ ~q?

The answer in this case is NO. If the antecedent of a conditional is false, then the consequent can be either true or false. Remember, "if it is raining, then I carry my umbrella." Now suppose it is NOT raining – does that mean you would NOT have your umbrella? No, you might carry it as a sunshield, or in case it rains later. So you cannot derive anything from a conditional and the *negation* of the *antecedent*. Consider the indirect truth table:

p → q   ~p   / q
F Ⓣ F   Ⓣ F   Ⓕ

On this truth value assignment, we have made the premises true while the conclusion is false. So the argument form is invalid.

Affirming the Consequent

If you know	$p \rightarrow q$
And you know	$\underline{q}$
Would you also know?	$\therefore p?$

This is also an INVALID form. If the consequent is true, the antecedent could be either true or false. Consider "if it is raining, I carry my umbrella." Now imagine that I have my umbrella. Does my carrying my umbrella necessarily imply that it is raining? Again, no, because I might carry it as a sunshade or in case of rain. So you cannot derive anything from a conditional and the *truth* of the *consequent*. Consider the indirect truth table:

$$\underline{p \rightarrow q} \qquad \underline{q} \qquad /\, p$$
$$F \,①\, T \qquad \quad ① \qquad ⑤$$

We have made the premises true while the conclusion is false, showing that this argument form is invalid. Be careful not to confuse Modus Ponens or Modus Tollens with denying the antecedent or affirming the consequent.

Disjunction Introduction (∨I) [11]

There is a rather odd rule in ND, called disjunction introduction. It says,

If you know	$\underline{p}$
You would also know (therefore)	$\therefore p \vee q$

This rule tells us that from any statement given as true, we can derive the *disjunction* of that statement with ANY other statement. This follows from the fact that a disjunction is true if *either* of the disjuncts is true. So, if a statement is given as true, the disjunction of that statement with any other

---

[11] This rule is sometimes referred to as "Addition (Add)."

statement (simple or compound) will be true. For instance, from the statement A given as true, we could derive any of the following statements:

A ∨ **B**
A ∨ (**B** & ~**C**)
A ∨ [(**F** ∨ **G**) & (~(**H** → **K**) ∨ (**L** & **M**))]

These statements may seem odd, but they follow directly from the rule that if either disjunct is true (in this case, A is true), the entire disjunction will be true.

4.5 – More Derivation Practice

Derivations in ND are a procedure of deriving the conclusion from the premises. ND is based on the fact that, in deductive arguments, the conclusion does not provide any new information – it is a restatement or re-ordering of the information given in the premises. Derivations in ND are a process of deriving information from the premises to show that the information contained in the conclusion is already contained in the premises.

This procedure often involves two related steps. First is the step of *analysis*. "Analysis" means "to break down." It involves using the rules to break down the given statements into simpler statements. The second step is the step of *synthesis*. "Synthesis" means "to put together." In this step, we take the simpler statements we derived from the given set and try to build them back up into the form that the conclusion has.

An analogy for this process may be helpful.[12] Imagine the initial set of statements as an object constructed with Lego pieces. What you need to do is break these pieces apart and construct a new object with the pieces. You cannot add any new pieces to the set (but you don't necessarily need to use all of the pieces in the new object) – the procedure is just to take the original object apart and build a new object with the parts.

Let's begin with a simple derivation. Consider this argument:

A & B
A → C
/∴ C

---

[12] As is always the case with analogies, if this analogy helps you, please use it. If it does not help you, dispense with it immediately.

To complete the derivation, we set up the premises of the argument as the given statements, and we place the conclusion to the right side of the last premise.

1. A & B   Given
2. A → C   Given   /∴ C

The first step is usually to look at the statements and see if there are any that can be broken down by the rules into simpler statements. The first statement is a conjunction. We can derive an A and/or a B from this statement by Conjunction Elimination. We don't necessarily need to derive both (but we can if we want); we only need to derive as much information as we need to complete the proof. Let's just derive the A for now:

1. A & B   Given
2. A → C   Given   /∴ C
3. A   1 &E

Now that we have the A, we can use it with B → C, and the rule Modus Ponens, to derive the C:

1. A & B   Given
2. A → C   Given   /∴ C
3. A   1 &E
4. C   2, 3 MP

We have now derived our conclusion from our premises, using the rules of the system. We have shown that if A & B and A → C are true, then C must be true as well. You could have derived a B at line 3 or 4 as well. That would be fine, but the B is not needed for any more derivations, so it doesn't need to be broken out of the conjunction.

Consider this argument:

1. A → D
2. D → ~F
3. A
4. E → F   /∴~E

Now we begin the process. There are several ways to approach a proof. We can begin by breaking down statements that we can see can be broken down. Often the best way to do this is to look for conjunctions or single statement letters (which can be derived from conjunctions), because they can be used to break down other more complex statements. Here we have an A in statement 3. Can we derive anything (or break any statements down) with an A? We can: We know A is true and we know that A → D (line 1). Modus Ponens thus allows us to derive D:

1. A → D	Given	
2. D → ~F	Given	
3. A	Given	
4. E → F	Given	/∴~E
5. D	1, 3 MP	

Now we have a D. Can we use that to derive anything (or break down any other statements)? We can, using Modus Ponens again, with line 2:

1. A → D	Given	
2. D → ~F	Given	
3. A	Given	
4. E → F	Given	/∴~E
5. D	1, 3 MP	
6. ~F	2, 5 MP[13]	

Now we have a ~F. Is there anything we can do with it? We have E → F in line 4. So we have a conditional and the negation of the consequent of the conditional. There is a rule that applies to this situation: Modus Tollens. It says that from a conditional and the negation of the consequent, we can derive the negation of the antecedent. So:

---

[13] Note carefully that this is MP, not MT. We have not derived the negation of the antecedent with the negation of the consequent. We have derived the consequent (it just happens to be a negated statement) from the antecedent.

1. $A \rightarrow D$	Given	
2. $D \rightarrow \sim F$	Given	
3. A	Given	
4. $E \rightarrow F$	Given	$/\therefore \sim E$
5. D	1, 3 MP	
6. $\sim F$	2, 5 MP	
7. $\sim E$	4, 6 MT	

Now we have derived the conclusion, so we are finished. This proof was primarily analysis, since the conclusion came about from breaking down the premises.

Building statements in proofs

Consider this argument:

1. $A \rightarrow D$	Given	
2. $(A \& D) \rightarrow E$	Given	
3. A	Given	
4. $E \rightarrow F$	Given	$/\therefore F$

We start by performing a Modus Ponens on lines 1 and 3:

1. $A \rightarrow D$	Given	
2. $(A \& D) \rightarrow E$	Given	
3. A	Given	
4. $E \rightarrow F$	Given	$/\therefore F$
5. D	1,3 MP	

Now look at line 2. It says that if A AND D are true (the conjunction of A and D), then E is true. Do we know that A AND D are true? We know that independently, from lines 3 and 5. Can we assert that the conjunction (A & D) is true? Yes. The rule Conjunction Introduction tells us that if we know that two statements are true independently, they can be put together as a conjunction. So on line 6 we can write:

1. A → D   Given
2. (A & D) → E   Given
3. A   Given
4. E → F   Given   /∴F
5. D   1,3 MP
6. A & D   3,5 &I

Now that we have formed the conjunction, we can derive the E and the F:

1. A → D   Given
2. (A & D) → E   Given
3. A   Given
4. E → F   Given   /∴F
5. D   1,3 MP
6. A & D   3,5 &I
7. E   2,6 MP
8. F   4,7 MP

This derivation shows analysis (breaking down) at lines 5, 7, and 8, and synthesis (putting together) at line 6.

Exercises

Derive the statements indicated using the basic ND rules.

A. 1. A → B   Given
    2. A   Given
    3. B → C   Given   /∴ C

B. 1. D ∨ E   Given
    2. ~D   Given
    3. E → F   Given   /∴F

C. 1. A → C   Given
    2. ~C   Given
    3. A ∨ B   Given   /∴B

D. 1. C ∨ E   Given
    2. ~E   Given
    3. C → ~D   Given
    4. D ∨ B   Given   /∴B

E. 1. C & D   Given
    2. C → E   Given
    3. D → F   Given
    4. (E & F) → G Given   /∴G

F. 1. J → K   Given
    2. K → L   Given
    3. L → M   Given
    4. M → N   Given
    5. J   Given   /∴N

G. 1. A ∨ B   Given
    2. ~A   Given
    3. B → ~C   Given
    4. D → C   Given   /∴~D

H. 1. ~A ∨ B Given
    2. ~B   Given
    3. C → A   Given
    4. C ∨ D   Given   /∴ D

I. 1. ~A ∨ ~B   Given
   2. A   Given
   3. C → B   Given
   4. <u>D → C</u>   Given   /∴~D

4.6 – The Rules of Replacement

Sometimes what is necessary in a proof is not breaking statements down or building new ones, but rearranging statements into different forms. There are a number of rules for doing this

We will write rules of replacement as

$$p \Leftrightarrow q$$

where $\Leftrightarrow$ means "can be replaced by". The double arrow means that the replacement can go either direction.

Some of the rules of replacement seem obvious, but help preserve the truth-preserving nature of the system:

Double Negation Elimination (~~E)

$$\sim\sim p \Leftrightarrow p$$

This is the same concept as in algebra – in a double negation, the two negatives cancel each other out. You can skip this step and just write double negations as non-negations in exercises.

Commutation (Comm)

$$(p \ \& \ q) \Leftrightarrow (q \ \& \ p)$$
$$(p \lor q) \Leftrightarrow (q \lor p)$$

Commutation states that the order of the statements in conjunctions and disjunctions doesn't affect the truth value of the statements (but this doesn't apply to conditionals!). Once established, statements can usually be treated this way without explicitly citing this rule.

Association (Ass)

$$[(p \ \& \ q) \ \& \ r] \Leftrightarrow [p \ \& \ (q \ \& \ r)]$$
$$[(p \lor q) \lor r] \Leftrightarrow [p \lor (q \lor r)]$$

Association states that the grouping of conjunctions and disjunctions does not affect the truth value of the statements (again, association doesn't apply to conditional statements!).

DeMorgan's Rules (DeM)

DeMorgan's rule is one of the most used and most important replacement rules. It comes into play in the following very common situation:

1. (A & B) → C   Given
2. ~C   Given

If we apply Modus Tollens to these lines, we have to derive the negation of the antecedent (A & B), so it would become ~(A & B). The problem is, there is no derivation rule that applies to negated conjunctions. Technically, this statement is a negation, not a conjunction. We can't get A or B (or ~A or ~B) out of the statement unless we think through more carefully what it means.

The statement ~(A & B) means "not (both) A AND B." That means that *not both* A and B are true. This, in turn, means that *at least one of the two is false*, or "A OR B is false." The symbolization for that statement would be (~A ∨ ~B).   Hence,

~(p & q) ⇔ (~p ∨ ~q)

This rule is similar to, but importantly different than, the algebra rule of distribution, which says -(a + b) = (-a + -b). In one sense, we are distributing the negation, but the SIGN has to change from dot to wedge.

A similar situation happens here:

1. (A ∨ B) → C   Given
2. ~C   Given

If we apply Modus Tolens at line 3, we get the negation of (A ∨ B), or ~(A ∨ B). Let's think through what this means. The statement says "NOT (A OR B)." This means, "Neither A NOR B is true" (this is where we get the word "neither" – it means NOT EITHER). If neither A nor B are true, then they're both false, or (~A AND ~B), or (~A & ~B). Hence,

~(p ∨ q) ⇔ (~p & ~q)

Negated Conditional Replacement (NCR)

Sometimes conditionals will be negated by MT as well;

1. $(A \rightarrow B) \rightarrow C$ Given
2. $\sim$C   Given

In this case, we would derive the negation of $(A \rightarrow B)$ on line 3, or $\sim(A \rightarrow B)$. But, there is no rule to deal with negated conditionals, so we will introduce one. There are two ways to derive this rule. First, from the truth table for a conditional, the conditional is false only in one case, when the antecedent is true, and the consequent is false; or, in this case, when A is true (A) AND B is false ($\sim$B). So we get a conjunction; (A & $\sim$B).

$$\sim(p \rightarrow q) \Leftrightarrow (p \text{ \& } \sim q)$$

4.6 – Some Common Derivation Strategies

Logicians look at derivations as puzzles (the popular game Sudoku is specifically a Natural Deduction derivation puzzle). The goal of puzzles is having them become harder and harder (similar to levels in video games). As derivations become more difficult, it becomes harder to see how to get from one line to the next. Here are several very common, but difficult, derivation strategies.

Wedge Introduction

Here is a short, but more advanced, problem:

1. A
2. $(A \vee B) \rightarrow C$ / ∴ C

We know we have to derive a C. From line 2, we can determine that if we can derive or construct the statement $(A \vee B)$, we can use MP to derive the C. But where does the $(A \vee B)$ come from? The answer is, line 1 plus Wedge Introduction. Many people find it very conceptually difficult to see this, so, if you do, don't worry. Just practice.

Line 1 tells us that A is true. We know that if one side of a wedge is true, the whole wedge will be true, *whatever is on the other side of it*. That means that we can add *anything we want* to the A as a disjunction, or a wedge. So, if A is true, then (A ∨ B) is *guaranteed* to be true (because the A makes it true, whatever the B is). So for line 3, we get:

1. A   Given
2. (A ∨ B) → C   Given   /∴C
3. A ∨ B   1 ∨I

Notice the justification. We are coming from line 1. Many people try to refer to line 2 in this justification, but that is incorrect. We are going to *use* line 3 with line 2 to derive the C. But line 3 does not come from or refer to line 2. It comes from line 1, using ∨I. Now that we have (A ∨ B) on line 3, we can use it to derive the C:

1. A   Given
2. (A ∨ B) → C   Given   /∴C
3. A ∨ B   1 ∨I
4. C   2,3 MP

Again, note the justification. Line 2 says that IF (A ∨ B) is true, THEN C is true. We have now derived that (A ∨ B) is true, on line 3, from line 1. So the step from 3 to 4 uses lines 2 (Given) and 3 (derived) to derive the C.

Reverse DeMorgan's and NCR

The origin of DeMorgan's' Rule and NCR is the case in which you have a compound statement negated by Modus Tollens. However, these rules can be used in reverse to construct statements as well. You have to know these rules very well to be able to see and use them this way. Here's an example:

1. ~A   Given
2. ~B   Given
3. ~(A ∨ B) → C   Given   /∴ C

We have to derive a C here. We know that IF ~(A ∨ B) is true, then C will be true. So we know that if we can derive or construct ~(A ∨ B), we can use it to derive the C. But how do we do that? Remember the rule for DeMorgan's:

~(p ∨ q) ⇔ (~p & ~q)

Notice that on the left side is ~(p ∨ q). That has the same form as what we want here. On the right side is (~p & ~q). Think about what that means. It means that IF we have the conjunction, (~p & ~q), we can *replace* it with ~(p ∨ q) (remember, replacement rules can work in either direction). It might help to reverse the order of the rule:

(~p & ~q) ⇔ ~(p ∨ q)

The application of this rule here is, if we can *derive* or *construct* (~A & ~B), we can use DeMorgan's (kind of in reverse) to derive ~(A ∨ B). Can we derive (~A & ~B)? Yes! Look at lines 1 and 2. They are, independently, ~A and ~B. Can we put together two independently true statements as a conjunction? Yes! Here is what it looks like:

1. ~A   Given
2. ~B   Given
3. ~(A ∨ B) → C   Given   / ∴ C
4. ~A & ~B   1,2 &I
5. ~(A ∨ B)   4 DeM

This is tricky, because it is a two-step process. First we have to construct the one side of the DeMorgan's setup (line 4), then use DeMorgan's to change it into the other form (line 5). Once we have ~(A ∨ B), we can use it to proceed with the proof – in this case it's only one more line, but often it is just one step in a longer derivation.

1. ~A   Given
2. ~B   Given
3. ~(A ∨ B) → C   Given   / ∴ C
4. ~A & ~B   1,2 &I
5. ~(A ∨ B)   4 DeM
6. C   3,5 MP

A similar process works with NCR. Here is a similar derivation using NCR. I won't explain each step this time; you should work your way through it and make sure you understand what is happening on each line:

1. A   Given
2. ~B   Given
3. ~(A → B) → C   Given   / ∴ C
4. A & ~B   1,2 &I
5. ~(A → B)   4 NCR
6. C   3,5 MP

Wedge Introduction plus DeM/NCR plus MT

This is one of the trickiest (and to logicians, funnest!) applications of these rules. Look at this problem:

1. ~A   Given
2. C → (A & B)   Given   / ∴ ~C

To see how to derive a ~C from these two lines is very difficult – it requires being able to think through several steps at once. It involves a strategy that is called the "reverse" strategy for doing proofs. The reverse strategy is abstract, but powerful (it is, conceptually, like indirect truth tables, which are also a form of reverse strategy). Here's how it works. We start with the conclusion, ~C. We ask, where would we derive a ~C from? Premise 2 is the only one with a C in it, so it would have to come from there. Premise 2 is a conditional with C as the antecedent. We ask, what rule would allow us to derive a ~C from a conditional with C as the antecedent? The answer is, Modus Tollens. It says if we have (p → q) and ~q we can derive the ~p. That means, if we have the negation of the consequent of the conditional (~q), we can derive the negation of the antecedent. What is the consequent of the conditional in line 2? It's (A & B). So, to derive the ~C, we have to derive or construct the negation of (A & B); ~(A & B). Let me show this (this method is a good method for doing the reverse strategy):

1. ~A   Given
2. C → (A & B)   Given   / ∴ ~C

   ~C   a. This is my goal; I'll use MT to get it
                         from line 2.

1. ~A   Given
2. C → (A & B)   Given   /∴ ~C

    ~(A & B)   b. If I can construct/derive this, I can use
                              MT to get ~C
    ~C   a. This is my goal; I'll use MT to get it
                              from line 2.

Now we can ask; is there a way to use what we have to
construct/derive ~(A & B)? Any time you need to construct/derive the
negation of a compound statement, you should think of reverse DeMorgan's
or NCR. Since we want the negation of a conjunction, it would have to be
reverse DeMorgan's. What would the other side of the equation be for a
DeMorgan's of ~(A & B)? It would be (~A ∨ ~B).

1. ~A   Given
2. C → (A & B)   Given   /∴ ~C

    ~A ∨ ~B   c. If I can construct/derive this, I can get to
                              ~(A & B) with DEM.
    ~(A & B)   b. If I can construct/derive this, I can use
                              MT to get ~C
    ~C   a. This is my goal; I'll use MT to get it
                              from line 2.

Now we can ask; is there a way to use what we have to
construct/derive ~A ∨ ~B? Line 1 is ~A. Can we use that? Yes! Remember
∨I – we can add anything we want to a true statement as a disjunction. To
get (~A ∨ ~B) from ~A, we just add it! That means we are done. We can
now go back and do line numbers and justifications:

1. ~A   Given
2. C → (A & B)   Given   /∴ ~C
3. ~A ∨ ~B   1 ∨I
4. ~(A & B)   3 DeM
5. ~C   2,4 MT

This is very abstract and complex thinking. That's what we're here to develop! There are a number of problems in the Exercise set that use this strategy; you should practice it and look for it. I remember it by thinking of the steps "wedge introduction plus DEM/NCR plus MT."

4.7 – Summary of ND Rules

Rules of Inference		Rules of Replacement[14]
&E p & q OR p & q ∴ p ∴ q	**&I** p q ∴ p & q	**DeM** ~(p ∨ q) ⇔ (~p & ~q) ~(p & q) ⇔ (~p ∨ ~q)
DS p ∨ q OR p ∨ q ~p ~q ∴ q ∴ p	**∨I** p ∴ p ∨ q	**NCR** ~(p → q) ⇔ (p & ~q)
MP p → q p ∴ q	**MT** p → q ~q ∴ ~p	

~B & ~C

~B → D

E → C   E → C

---

[14] I have not included Double Negation, Association or Commutation in this set; they will not be necessary in the exercises.

Exercises

Derive the following statements from the sets given. Watch especially for Disjunction Introduction (∨I), DeMorgan's, and NCR and be careful with negated statements.

A. 1. A → B
    2. A
    3. B → (C & D)
    4. D → E   /∴ E

B. 1. (D → A) & (C → B)
    2. ~A
    3. ~B   /∴ ~D & ~C

C. 1. [(D & (E ∨ F)) → G] ∨ B
    2. ~(B ∨ G)
    3. D & (H → (E ∨ F)) /∴ ~H

D. 1. A
    2. (A ∨ B) → C
    3. C → D   /∴ D

E. 1. E
    2. [(E ∨ M) & (F ∨ Q)] → G
    3. F   /∴ G

F. 1. A → (B & C)
    2. A
    3. (B ∨ E) → D   /∴ D

G. 1. (B ∨ C) → D
    2. ~D
    3. B ∨ E
    4. C ∨ F   /∴ E & F

H. 1. (A ∨ B) → C
    2. ~C
    3. D → A
    4. B ∨ E   /∴ ~D & E

I. 1. M
    2. (M ∨ N) → ~(P & Q)
    3. P & (R → Q)   /∴ ~R

J. 1. (A & B) → C
    2. ~C & A
    3. D → B   /∴ ~D

K. 1. (A ∨ B) → ~(C ∨ D)
    2. A
    3. D ∨ E
    4. (E ∨ Z) → F   /∴ F

L. 1. ~A & ~B
    2. ~(A ∨ B) → ~(C ∨ D)
    3. C ∨ E
    4. ~F → D
    5. (E & F) → G   /∴ G

M. 1. ~A & ~B
    2. (C & D) → (A ∨ B)
    3. D   /∴ ~C

N. 1 ~A
    2. ~(A & B) → C   /∴ C

O. 1. ~A
   2. (C ∨ D) → (A & B)
   3. (F & G) → (C ∨ D)
   4. F   ∴~G

P. 1. (B & C) → (E & F)
   2. ~E
   3. B
   4. ~C → D   /∴ D

Q. 1. (A → B) → C
   2. ~C
   3. A → D
   4. E → B
   5. (D & ~B) → F   /∴ F

R. 1. A
   2. ~B
   3. C → (A → B)
   4. C ∨ D   /∴ D

S. 1. [(A ∨ B) → C] → D
   2. ~(D ∨ A)   /∴ B

T. 1. [(A & B) ∨ (~B ∨ ~D)] → (E & F)
   2. ~E   /∴ ~(D → A)

U. 1. (~A ∨ B) → C
   2. D → (A → B)

   3. ~C   /∴ ~D

V. 1. ~A
   2. (A → B) → (C → A)
   3. C ∨ D   /∴ D

W. 1. B → C
   2. ~(A → C)
   3. D → (A → B)   /∴ ~D

X. 1. (A & (B → C)) → D
   2. ~E → C
   3. ~(A → D)   /∴ E

Y. 1. ((A ∨ B) → C) → ((E & (F & G))
   2. B → C
   3. ~E   /∴ A

Chapter 5: Inductive Logic

5.1 – Inductive Inferences

If you remember from the opening section, arguments are divided into categories depending on the type and strength of the inference between the premises and the conclusion. Here is the chart of possible inferences:

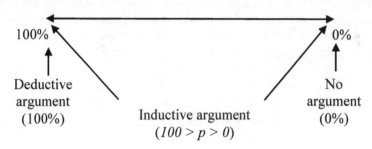

Strength of Inferences

We have been studying deductive arguments, in which the premises are intended to support the conclusion in an absolute way; that is, the truth of the premises guarantees the truth of the conclusion, absolutely. Categorical Logic, Sentential Logic, and Natural Deduction, are all branches of deductive logic.

Now consider the argument:

Most people who drive Jaguar cars are rich.
Bob drives a Jaguar car.
Therefore, Bob is rich.

In this argument, even if we take the premises to be true, there is no attempt to demonstrate absolutely that Bob is rich. The attempt is only to make the reader think it is *probable* that Bob is rich (the key here is the word "most" in the first premise is the key word). There is an attempt at persuasion here, but not in an absolute sense. Arguments in which the arguer only intends to give *probabilistic* support for the conclusion (that is, they try to show that the conclusion is probably, not necessarily, true) are called **INDUCTIVE** arguments. Inductive arguments that make the conclusion very probable are more convincing, or better, arguments, while inductive arguments that don't make the conclusion very probable are less convincing and worse arguments.

Evaluating Inductive arguments

The process of evaluating inductive arguments is parallel to the process of evaluating deductive arguments. First, we will evaluate the inference; the inference. Then we will evaluate the truth of the premises. Just like in deductive arguments, if the argument fails the first test, there is no need to do the second test.

The evaluation of the inference in an inductive argument is parallel to, but slightly different than, the evaluation of the inference in a deductive argument. In an inductive argument, we are evaluating the *probability* of the conclusion, given (assuming) the truth of the premises. The question here is not "is it possible for the conclusion to be false" (because it is ALWAYS possible for the conclusion to be false in inductive arguments). The question is, "given these premises," how likely is it that the conclusion is true?

Consider the following argument:

97% of home-owners in Los Angeles County irrigate their lawns.
Bill owns a home in Los Angeles County.
Therefore, Bill irrigates his lawn.

If we assume these premises to be true, is it probable that the conclusion would be true as well? In this case it is very probable (about 97%). We would say, then, that the inference is *strong* in this argument.

Now consider this argument:

I know 3 people who own Jaguars (cars), and they all make over
    $250,000 per year.
There's a Jaguar next to me on the freeway.
Therefore, its owner must make over $250,000 per year.

In this case, if we assume that the premises are true, they give very weak support for the conclusion. The arguer knows only 3 people who own Jaguars, and this is a very small test group to make the generalization that someone else who owns a Jaguar would have a similar income. The inference in this case is very *weak*.

It is an interesting and difficult question in inductive logic, "what is the dividing line between strong and weak arguments?" The official dividing line is 50% probability. But this is very ambiguous. Is an argument that makes the conclusion 51% probable really strong? Is an argument that makes the conclusion 49% probable really weak? This is one of the problems that makes logicians prefer deductive arguments. Deductive arguments are valid or invalid, and there's no middle ground! Evaluating the strength of inductive arguments is very difficult. One way to think about the evaluation is to use betting as a test. Think "would I be wise to bet money on the conclusion being true, given these premises?" If not, it is probably not a very strong argument. Here are several things to keep in mind:

1. I will try to give you arguments that are pretty obviously strong or weak.
2. I am more interested in your REASONS for thinking arguments are strong or weak than your answer of "strong" or "weak" itself.
3. Just use "greater than 50%" and "less than 50%" as your cut-off. Even if an argument is just over 50%, we'll call it strong for our purposes (but see #1).

The second step of evaluation is exactly the same as for deductive arguments: we evaluate the **truth** of the premises. As with deductive arguments, if has failed the inference test, this step is unnecessary. An argument must pass both tests to be a good argument, so if it has already failed the first test, there is no need to proceed to the second step. In this step, we simply ask whether ALL of the premises are true. Consider this argument,

>85% of humans have 2 heads.
>John is a human.
>Therefore, John has 2 heads.

Note that the inference in this argument is strong. ***IF the premises were true, it WOULD be probable (85%) that John would have 2 heads***. However, it is not true that 85% of humans have two heads. An argument that has any false premises is **UNCOGENT**, and an argument that has all true premises is **COGENT.**

The following chart outlines the process for evaluating inductive arguments.

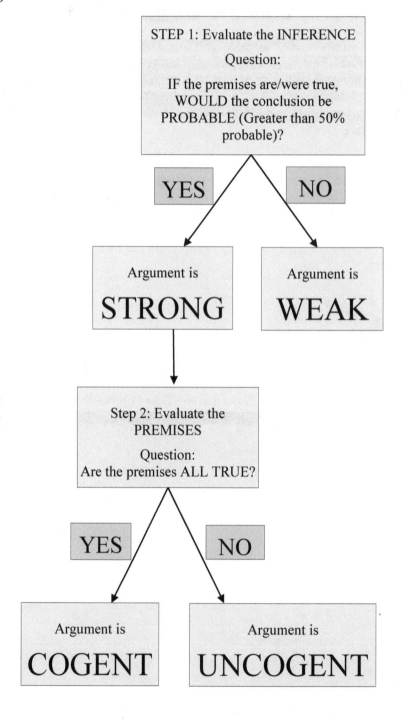

Exercises

The following inductive arguments have very common inductive argument forms. See if you can identify the kind of argument each is (you won't be tested on this). Then, for each argument, answer these questions:
  1. Assign a probability to the conclusion, based on the premises (i.e., "this conclusion is ____% probable, based on these premises). Explain why you chose that number. Is the argument strong or weak? (NOTE: I am more interested in the number you give the probability and your reasons for giving the number than I am on the answer "strong" or "weak").
  2. Is the argument cogent or uncogent? Why? (If you're not sure whether statements are true or not, just choose one and state that in your answer. If statements are about imaginary people, take them to be true.)

1. My brother said that the democrats are sure to win the next election. Therefore, the democrats will win.
2. Michael Jordan (the famous basketball player) said on a TV ad: "Hanes underwear are the best." So Hanes underwear must be the best.
3. A Gallup poll reported that 67% of Americans favor abolishing the death penalty. Therefore, my neighbor Sally would support abolishing the death penalty.
4. 80% of the bald people in the world are men. Pat is bald. Therefore, Pat is a man.
5. 80% of humans are over 10 feet tall. Pat is a human. Therefore, Pat is over 10 feet tall.
6. I left my car headlights on last night. Therefore, this morning, my car battery will be dead.
7. Every fall, during the month of September, Canadian geese fly over my house headed southward. It is now September. I expect to see the geese any day now.
8. Every January, a herd of elephants migrates through Los Angeles, headed for Mexico. It is now January. We should expect to see the herd of elephants any day now.
9. A whole school of sardines got stranded in Long Beach Harbor and died last month. We should expect to see schools of sardines dying in the harbor every month now.
10. Bob was just honorably discharged from the Navy Seals and is healthy. He can do 100 pushups easily. Bill was also just honorably discharged from the Navy Seals and is healthy. He'll be able to do 100 pushups as well.
11. When a black cat crosses your path, it causes you to have particularly good luck. A black cat crossed my path this morning. So I'm expecting good luck any time.

Chapter 6: Informal Fallacies

6.1 – Introduction

The main area of study in inductive logic is referred to as "Informal Fallacies." The exact meaning of the phrase "informal fallacy" is somewhat ambiguous. "Fallacy" is not ambiguous – it refers to any error in reasoning. It is based on the same root word as "false" and "fallacious." "Informal" *is* ambiguous – it might refer to the fact that these "fallacies" are related to inductive or informal logic (as opposed to deductive or formal logic). Or it might refer to the fact that these fallacy patterns are very common types of arguments forms that we encounter in life. The best definition of the term is "common errors in human reasoning." According to Wikipedia, informal fallacies are "arguments that are fallacious for reasons other than structural (formal) flaws and which usually require examination of the argument's content."

Since a fallacy is an error in reasoning, it is helpful to begin by defining good reasoning, or a good argument. We have looked at several specific tests of arguments, related to validity, soundness, strength, and cogency. Now we're going to consider a *less* specific definition. For the purpose of studying fallacies, we will understand "good argument" to mean *"an argument that presents sufficient true, relevant evidence to make the conclusion probable."* This definition covers all of the specific ideas we have covered, and provides two additional criteria that we will consider; sufficiency and relevance. Those mean that the evidence presented to you must be sufficient (there must be enough of it) and relevant (it must be related to and support the conclusion), before you are convinced by it. Most informal fallacies fail at either relevance or sufficiency.

One final note must be made: a common, but incorrect definition of "good argument" is "an argument that convinces lots of people." The problem with this definition is that many bad arguments convince lots of people! An argument that convinces lots of people may be effective, but it is not good in the sense that we intend it here. We mean "logically good."

There is a very large number of informal fallacies. Wikipedia lists about 80. The web site *fallacyfiles.org* lists well over 100. Fallacies are not grouped in any particular way, since there are so many different ones. Here we will study the 20 that I find to be the most common, sorted more-or-less alphabetically.

The first group of fallacies we will consider are actually a group. They are called "Appeal Fallacies." Technically, a good argument must appeal to your reason and not anything else. These fallacies are called appeal fallacies because they *appeal* to something other than the listener's reason. The problem is, since the information given by the arguer is not aimed at your reason, it ends up being irrelevant – in our definition, relevant evidence means "evidence that appeals to reason and is directed at this conclusion."

6.2 – Argument forms that are always bad

Appeal to pity

Consider the following scenario. You get stopped by a police officer for speeding. When the police office approaches your window, you begin crying and say, "but officer, I can't get a ticket. If I get a ticket I'll lose my license and then I will lose my job and I'll have to move back in with my parents, who I don't get along with!" What are you doing in this situation? First, you're trying to convince the officer of something (I shouldn't get a ticket). That means you're making an argument. Is it a good argument? Remember, the issue here isn't *effectiveness* – you might very well convince the officer not to give you a ticket. The issue is, did you provide sufficient relevant evidence that the officer shouldn't give you a ticket? The answer in this case is "No." Speeding tickets are about whether you broke the law or not. The information about your license and your job and your parents is all irrelevant – it's not about the issue of whether you were speeding. So you are not appealing to the police officer's reason. What are you appealing to? You're trying to make the office feel sorry for you, or you are appealing to an emotion; *pity*.

Any time the point of an argument is to get the other person to accept a conclusion because they feel a certain way, you are committing an appeal to emotion fallacy. There is a separate fallacy name for each emotion one might appeal to. This case would be an *appeal to pity*.

In general, I will give you fallacy definitions in a couple of steps. I will identify the FORM of the fallacy – what is happening in the argument, and the FALLACY – what is wrong with the argument form being used. For "appeal to pity" it would be:

A) Form: Arguer tries to make audience feel sorry for her/him.
B) Fallacy: Feelings are irrelevant to the strength of an argument.

When it comes to evaluating informal fallacies, a complete evaluation consists of 4 parts:

1. A statement of what the conclusion is. In informal settings, arguers are often very ambiguous about what their conclusion is. One of the best ways to identify a conclusion is to ask yourself: "what does this person want from me (or their audience)." People make arguments because they want something from you.

Some notes about conclusion:
  ⅄ Conclusions should always be written as statements.
  ⅄ An argument, technically, can have only one conclusion.
  ⅄ The word "because" is never part of a conclusion. "Because" indicates evidence FOR the conclusion, but that's not part of the conclusion.
2. A short description of how the arguer tries to convince the listener to accept the conclusion.
3. An analysis of whether the argument is a good argument or not, based on our definition of "good argument." Does the arguer give sufficient, relevant, true evidence that makes the conclusion probable?
4. The name of the fallacy committed, if one is.

For our first example, the complete answer would be something like:
1. The conclusion of this argument is "I shouldn't get a ticket".
2. The person tries to convince the officer by trying to make the officer feel sorry for him/her.
3. This is a bad argument – the reasons given are irrelevant.
4. This is an appeal to pity fallacy.

With this introduction to informal fallacies, I will now introduce the rest of the fallacies with the form/fallacy information, followed by an example and an analysis using this 4-step approach.

Appeal to fear

A) Form: Arguer threatens to harm the listener.
B) Fallacy: A threat is irrelevant to the strength of an argument.

Example: Student to teacher: I deserve a better grade in this course. I have some cell-phone pictures of you drinking with your students at the bar last weekend.

Analysis:
1. Conclusion: I should get a better grade.
2. The arguer tries to convince the teacher by (implicitly) threatening him or her with reporting him or her for drinking with students.
3. This is a bad argument – the information given is irrelevant – it has nothing to do with what grade the student deserves.
4. This is an appeal to force fallacy.

Appeal to consequences

A) Form: The arguer refers to positive or negative consequences in order to argue that a certain action is good or bad or right or wrong.

B) Fallacy: This is a controversial issue. Are the consequences of an action what determine its moral value? Some people think so. Other say that it is possible to have a morally bad action with good consequences (if I kidnap someone and do medical experiments on them but I end up curing cancer, that would be an action with good consequences, but most people say it would still be morally wrong to kidnap and experiment on someone) and a morally good action with bad consequences (if I give up a kidney to save my son's life and something goes wrong and my son and I both die, those are very bad consequences, but it was still morally good to give a kidney). Because of these kinds of situations, these people say that consequences ALONE cannot determine whether an action is good or bad. If you accept this, then to appeal to the consequences of an action is irrelevant or not sufficient to justify it.

Example: We should continue with more advanced stem-cell research – just think of all of the medical breakthroughs it could lead to.

Analysis:
1. Conclusion: We should continue with more advanced stem-cell research.
2. The person arguer to convince the audience by appealing to the good consequences stem-cell research might have.
3. Whether this is a good argument or not depends on whether you believe that good consequences can justify any action. But if you believe this, you have to be willing to accept things like me kidnapping you and doing medical experiments on you to cure cancer!
4. If you don't think that consequences can justify any action, this is an appeal to consequences fallacy.

Appeal to ignorance

A) Forms:
      i.   X has not been proven true, so X is false.
      ii.   X has not been proven false, so X is true.

B) Fallacy: lack of proof does not constitute proof.

Example: Extraterrestrial life has never been proven to exist. So it must not exist. OR Extraterrestrial life has never been proven to be impossible. So it must exist.

Analysis:
1. Conclusion: ET life does or doesn't exist.
2. The arguer supports the conclusion by stating that the other position is not proven.
3. This is a bad argument. Lack of proof for one position does not constitute proof of the other position.
4. This is an appeal to ignorance fallacy.

Appeal to novelty

A) Form: Arguer claims that the conclusion is true because it is new or modern, OR that an idea is false because it is old or traditional.
B) Fallacy: The fact that an idea is new or modern does not in itself prove that it is correct. For instance, the idea that the earth is flat was new and modern at one point!

Example: We must accept that the mind and the brain are the same thing. After all, that's what modern science says (or, after all, the belief that they are separate is an ancient belief).

Analysis:
1. Conclusion: The mind and the brain are the same thing.
2. The arguer supports the conclusion by stating that the conclusion is the "new" or "modern" idea and that the other position is "old" or "ancient."
3. This is a bad argument. This doesn't mean that the conclusion is false, it only means that the fact that the idea is "new" or "modern" does not in itself prove that it is true.
4. This is an appeal to novelty fallacy.

Appeal to tradition

A) Form: This fallacy is the reverse of appeal to novelty. Arguer claims that their conclusion is true because it is old or traditional, OR that an idea is false because it is new or modern.
B) Fallacy: The fact that an idea is old or traditional does not in itself prove that it is correct. For instance, the idea that the earth is flat is old, but it is not true!

Example: We must accept that humans have souls in addition to their bodies. After all, that's what people have always believed.

1. Conclusion: Humans have souls in addition to their bodies.
2. The arguer supports the conclusion by stating that the conclusion is what people "have always believed."
3. This is a bad argument. This doesn't mean that the conclusion is false, it only means that the fact that the idea is old or that people have believed it does not in itself prove that it is true.
4. This is an appeal to tradition fallacy.

Appeal to the people

A) Form: Arguer claims that their conclusion is true because lots of people believe it.
B) Fallacy: The fact that "lots" of people believe an idea to be true does not make it true. For instance, lots of people once believed the earth was flat, but it wasn't true. And lots of Americans once believed that slavery was morally okay, but that wasn't true.

Example: We should all accept that abortion in the third trimester is morally okay. The majority of Americans believe it.

Analysis:
1. Conclusion: abortion in the third trimester is morally okay.
2. The arguer supports the conclusion by stating that the majority of Americans believe this.
3. This is a bad argument. That doesn't mean the conclusion is false, it only means that the fact that a majority of Americans believe it does not in itself mean that it is correct.
4. This is an appeal to the people.

Ad hominem - argument against the person

"Ad hominem" is a set of fallacies in which the arguer attacks the person making another argument, in order to convince the listener to reject the other person's argument. They are arguments against arguments. The conclusion in an ad hominem argument is always to reject what the other person is saying.

Ad hominem abusive – direct attack on person's character - "character assassination"

A) Form: You should reject person A's argument, because person A has a bad character

B) Fallacy: Ad hominem abusive break our "always bad" criterion, because, while they are *almost* always bad arguments, they can sometimes be good or strong arguments. Usually, and what makes this form a fallacy, a person's character is not relevant to the strength of his or her argument.

Example: Senator Brown has said that we need to cut spending on medical programs because of the economic situation. But Brown is a real idiot. It is well known that he parties all the time and sleeps with prostitutes. We shouldn't listen to Brown.

Analysis:
1. Conclusion: We should reject what Brown says about spending on medical programs.
2. The person tries to convince the listener by discussing bad things that Brown supposedly does or has done (without any real evidence that they are true).
3. This is a bad argument – whether or not the information given about Brown is true, it is irrelevant because it is unrelated to the issue of the economy or spending on medical programs.
4. This is an ad hominem abusive fallacy.

Ad hominem circumstantial – attack on person's motives

A) Form: You should reject person A's argument, because person A has ulterior motives

B) Fallacy: Person A's motives are not relevant to the strength of Person A's argument. Ad hominem circumstantial arguments are tricky. It is quite possible that a person's motives can make you doubt that they're presenting a good argument. But, technically, the motives for making an argument are irrelevant with respect to the strength of the argument itself. As reasoners, we must always evaluate the evidence in the argument, not the reasons for the argument.

Example: The oil company BP is saying that they should not be held accountable for the explosion that caused the oil spill in Texas. But of course BP would say that. They're going to have to pay billions of dollars to clean it up if they're found guilty.

Analysis:
1. Notice that this argument doesn't even have a stated conclusion. This is very common in informal arguments. It is clear what the arguer intends, though – they think BP should be held accountable for the explosion. The conclusion is: reject what BP is saying about NOT being held accountable.
2. The arguer tries to convince the audience by questioning the motives BP might have for not wanting to be held accountable for the oil spill.
3. This is a bad argument – the reasons given are irrelevant. The issue is not what BP wants or doesn't want, but what evidence there is that they as a company were primarily responsible for the explosion.
4. This is an ad hominem circumstantial fallacy.

Non-fallacious ad hominem
A) If Person A's character, motives, or actions do affect the strength of their argument, then there is no fallacy.

Example: Senator Brown has said that we need to cut spending on medical programs because of the financial situation. But Brown is a bad fiscal planner. I can give you three examples of times when he has made proposals to cut spending that have had very bad fiscal consequences for the state. We should not listen to Brown's ideas.

Analysis:
1. Conclusion: We should reject Brown's ideas about spending on medical programs.
2. The arguer tries to convince the listener by citing times when Brown has given bad fiscal advice.
3. This is an okay argument – If Brown has been wrong on several occasions about his fiscal predictions, that makes it reasonable to conclude that he might be wrong in this case. Still, it would be stronger if the arguer talked about the actual policies Brown is suggesting and how they will not work out, rather than attack Brown's character.
4. This is an ad hominem abusive argument– but it's not a fallacy.

Accident – faulty rule application

A) Form: A general rule is applied to a specific situation
B) Fallacy: The general rule doesn't apply to this particular situation

Example: It is illegal to drive 100 miles per hour on city streets. Therefore, that police officer was doing something illegal when she drove 100 miles per hour chasing that bank robber.

Analysis:
1. Conclusion: The police officer was doing something illegal.
2. The arguer supports the conclusion by citing the law against driving 100 miles per hour on city streets.
3. This is a bad argument; the law does not apply to police officers chasing criminals.
4. This is an accident fallacy.

Begging the Question (circular argument)

A) Form: The arguer assumes the truth of the conclusion and/or presents it as one of the premises
B) Fallacy: The premises are supposed to provide evidence for the truth of the conclusion, not state the conclusion.

Example 1: We should believe god exists because the Bible (or the Koran or the Torah or the Bhagavad Gita) says he exists. And we should believe what the Bible (or the Koran or the Torah or the Bhagavad Gita) is true because it is god's word.

Analysis:
1. There are two arguments with two conclusions here. One is "god exists", the other is "the Bible (Koran...) is true."
2. The arguer supports each conclusion by referring to the other conclusion.
3. The arguments are both bad. That doesn't mean that the ideas are not true. It just means that there is not sufficient INDEPENDENT EVIDENCE given for either one. The holy book supports god's existence and god's existence supports the holy book. This is arguing in a circle; hence the name.
4. This is a (begging the question) circular argument.

Example 2: Why am I a Republican? Because Republicans are the answer to our nation's problems!

Analysis:
1. There is not really a conclusion or an argument here at all. To "be a Republican" (or Democrat) and to think that Republicans (or Democrats) are "the answer to our nation's problems" are really the

same thing. So the arguer has really just restated the same idea as a premise and a conclusion both.

2.   The arguer argues by restating the same idea as a premise and a conclusion.
3.   The argument is weak (actually non-existent). There is no factual evidence presented to explain or support what Republicans actually believe or why it's "the answer to our nation's problems."
4.   This is a (begging the question) circular argument.

Begging the Question (Assumed/suppressed evidence)

A) Form: The arguer doesn't present important evidence or assumes the truth of one or more of the premises (when its truth is not obvious). There is a strong connection between assumed/suppressed evidence and enthymemes in Categorical Logic. Enthymemes are particular cases of assumed/suppressed evidence.
B) Fallacy: The premises are supposed to be clearly true (or they must be established by more arguments) and all of the evidence (both positive and negative) must be presented.

Example 1: Why is abortion wrong? Because all murder is wrong.

Analysis:
1.   Conclusion: Abortion is wrong.
2.   The arguer supports the conclusion by stating that all murder is wrong.
3.   This is a weak argument. The arguer assumes but suppresses (doesn't state) the main controversial claim – that abortion is murder. Whether you believe this or not, just stating or assuming it doesn't make it true.
4.   This is a (begging the question) assumed/suppressed evidence fallacy.

Example 2: Why is abortion okay? Because women have the right to do what they want with their own bodies, that's why.

Analysis:
1.   Conclusion: Abortion is okay.
2.   The arguer supports the conclusion by stating that women have the right to do what they want with their bodies.
3.   This is a weak argument. The arguer assumes but suppresses (doesn't state) the main controversial claim – that a fetus is (just) a part of woman's body with no independent rights of its own.

Whether you believe this or not, just stating or assuming it doesn't make it true.
4. This is a (begging the question) assumed/suppressed evidence fallacy.

Complex question

A) Form: A question is posed that already assumes what he questioner is trying to establish. These are related to our phrase "damned if you do, damned if you don't."
B) Fallacy: Any answer will implicate the person questioned, because the question assumes and is posed to force the responder to admit the charge.

Example: "Have you stopped beating your wife?"

Analysis:
1. Conclusion: You beat your wife.
2. The arguer supports the conclusion by phrasing the question in a way that forces the responder to admit that it's true.
3. This is a weak argument. The arguer assumes that the person beats his wife.
4. This is a (begging the question) complex question fallacy.

Missing the point

A) Form: The arguer draws a conclusion that is entirely different from the one suggested by the premises.
B) Fallacy: The relevance of the premises is directed to a conclusion other than the one presented.

Example: The Space Shuttle fleet is now old and the shuttles can no longer be operated within an acceptable margin of safety. I guess we'll have to make the astronauts sign releases saying that they accept all the risks of flying them.

Analysis:
1. Conclusion: Make the astronauts sign releases to fly the Space Shuttles.
2. The arguer supports this conclusion by describing the age and condition of the shuttles
3. This is a bad argument. The odd thing here is that the evidence is good; but the conclusion drawn is the wrong conclusion! The

obvious conclusion (and the actual one that NASA reached) is, stop flying them!
4. This is a missing the point fallacy.

Naturalistic fallacy

A) Form: The arguer supports a point by saying that it is "natural" or "found in nature." Naturalistic arguments are usually moral arguments.

B) Fallacy: The fact that an activity is found in nature has no bearing on whether it is good or bad. If "found in nature" meant "good," all of these things (and may others) would be good (because they are all found in nature): eating your offspring, rape and torture.

Example 1: Having multiple sexual partners is morally okay because it is very common in nature.

Analysis:
1. Conclusion: Having multiple sexual partners is morally okay.
2. The arguer supports his or her point by saying the activity is found in nature.
3. This is a weak argument. That doesn't mean that the conclusion is false; it just means that saying "it is found in nature" does not provide sufficient support to make the conclusion probable. Many morally wrong things are found in nature.
4. This is a naturalistic fallacy.

Example 2: Homosexual activity is wrong because it is unnatural.

Analysis:
1. Conclusion: Homosexual behavior is wrong.
2. The arguer supports her or his point by saying the behavior is "unnatural."
3. This is a weak argument. "Unnatural" is not defined, so it is unclear what it means. If it means "not found in nature" then it is false – homosexual behavior is found in nature.
4. This is a naturalistic fallacy. Whatever "unnatural" means, it is not relevant or sufficient to make the conclusion probable. It is probably also a begging the question, suppressed evidence fallacy, since "unnatural" is not defined, so not all the relevant evidence has been presented.

Straw Man and Red Herring

Straw Man and Red Herring fallacies are two of the oldest and commonest informal fallacies. They have similar forms. They are like the ad hominem arguments in that they are arguments against someone else's argument, so their conclusions will be "reject Person A's argument." They are similar to each other in that in both cases, the arguers *misrepresents* the argument of the other person, then tries to use the misrepresented argument to defeat the real argument. But in fact, in both cases, the arguer is not talking about the real argument at all!

Straw Man
   A) Form
      1. Arguer distorts the argument of his/her opponent
      2. Arguer attacks distorted argument, rather than the real argument
   B) Fallacy - What's being attacked is not the real argument, and is usually irrelevant with respect to the real argument (although it is usually related)

Example: President Obama argues that we should have a national health care plan. Well here's what I think he wants. He wants to make the U.S. a socialist country. He wants to impose so many taxes on us hard-working Americans that we won't be able to make a decent living. Take the money from the hard workers and give it to the lazy members of society. That's what Obama wants! Don't do it!

Analysis:
1. Conclusion: Reject Obama's argument about national health care.
2. The arguer tries to convince us by saying that Obama wants to impose socialism and lots of taxes.
3. This is a bad argument – the evidence given is false and irrelevant. The arguer is taking national health care and distorting the issue to be about socialism and high taxes. Notice that socialism and high taxes are *related* to national health care, they're just not what Obama has talked about. It's very unlikely that Obama wants socialism.
4. This is a straw man fallacy.

Red Herring
   A) Form:
      1. Arguer leads the discussion away from the real argument altogether. The name of this fallacy comes from the practice of training bloodhounds. One of the tests is to drag a red herring (a smelly fish) across the track that the dog is following, to try

to get it to leave the track and follow a different one. So think of Red Herrings as "leading off track" arguments.
2.   Arguer may or may not attack the real argument
B) Fallacy – The presented premises have nothing to do with the real argument

Example: Senator Brown argues that we should not raise the national speed limit to 75 mph. But this is wrong. Cars today are much more efficient than they have ever been, and can go 100 mph without a problem. These new aluminum engines can produce more horsepower than the old cast iron engines with only half the weight.

Analysis:
1. Conclusion: Reject Brown's argument about raising the national speed limit.
2. The arguer tries to convince the listener of his conclusion by talking about how efficient and light new cars are.
3. This is a bad argument – the reasons given are irrelevant. The issues regarding speed limits are gas consumption and safety. Lighter, more efficient cars may reduce gas consumption (although this is not stated), but nothing is said about safety at all.
4. This is a red herring fallacy.

Exercises

Use the 4-step analysis method to evaluate these arguments. Some of them are NOT fallacies.

1. Mary is a figure skater. Most figure skaters are physically fit. Therefore, Mary is physically fit.
2. Mary is a bad figure skater because she falls down during every performance, has never won a medal, and is not graceful.
3. Bill says we should support his investment program. But Bill was arrested last year for beating his wife. Therefore, we should reject Bill's advice.
4. Bill says that we should support his investment program. He says that he knows we cheated on our taxes last year and that he has a good friend in the IRS.
5. Bill says that we should support his investment program, because if we don't, he'll lose all the money he's invested in it and will go bankrupt.
6. Bill says we should support his investment program. But Bill is a fraud. He has been in jail twice for promoting phony investment schemes. Therefore, we should reject Bill's advice.

7. Bill says that we should invest in his investment program. But I don't think it's such a good idea. The stock market is a volatile enterprise. It has gone up and down over and over through its lifetime. Sometimes it's up and sometimes it's down. It has crashed at least twice that we know of.

8. Bill says we should invest in his investment program because everyone he knows has invested.

9. Bill says that we should invest in his investment program. He's using the latest economic theories so it's sure to succeed.

10. Bill's investment program is going to fail because he has not thought it out clearly, he has no concept of basic economics, and he doesn't know anything about the stock market.

11. American Express ad: You're in a strange city. You've been robbed. What will you do? Who will you turn to? Carry American Express.

12. A wine ad shows a room full of shiny, happy people, all drinking wine. The caption says, "Gallo – a part of your life." This is an argument – evaluate it.

13. It can't be so wrong for me to have the occasional affair. After all, almost no animals in nature are strictly monogamous.

14. It can't be so wrong for me to cheat on my boyfriend occasionally, so long as her never finds out about it. It's not hurting anyone.

15. Marriage has always been defined as between a man and a woman. That's enough reason to keep it that way.

16. The idea that marriage must be between a man and a woman is ancient and outdated. We have to get our laws up to date.

17. There is no strong argument for keeping marriage limited to opposite genders. So it's time to change it.

18. There is no strong argument for changing the definition of marriage. So we have to keep it what it is.

19. Why should gay marriage be allowed? Because there's nothing wrong with it, that's why!

20. Abortion should be allowed because lots of women will go out and have abortions anyway, and many will be harmed by illegal back-alley abortions.

21. Senator Jones says that we should raise taxes to help balance the budget. But we all know what Senator Jones is up to. She just wants to be re-elected and she knows that she won't be re-elected if she doesn't vote for increased taxes.

22. Senator Jones says that we should raise taxes to help balance the budget. And she is right. Raising taxes will help balance the budget.

6.3 – Informal argument forms that may be strong or weak

The following set of argument forms is a slightly different set. The argument forms we have looked at are, except for a few special cases, *always* fallacies, or always bad arguments. The next set is a set of common inductive argument patterns that *may or may not* be fallacies – they can be either strong or weak arguments. This makes the analysis somewhat more complex, because in addition to identifying the pattern or form, you must evaluate whether the presented argument is strong or weak.

Argument from Authority

A) Form: The arguer cites a person as evidence that a claim is true or false.

B) Evaluation: Arguments from authority can be strong or weak. The issue is, is this person a credible, knowledgeable source regarding this issue? If so, then the argument is relatively strong. If not, it is relatively weak.

Example 1: The FDA has declared that dietary supplement "Xanthrin Pro" has had problematic side effects in a significant number of users. Therefore, you should stop taking it.

Analysis:
1. Conclusion: Stop taking Xanthrin Pro.
2. The arguer cites the FDA's statement regarding problematic side effects.
3. This argument is relatively strong. It is the business of the FDA to evaluate products and warn people about dangers. Is it certain that YOU will have these side effects if YOU take the supplement? No. But remember, these are inductive arguments, not deductive. Would you be wise to take the supplement after an FDA warning? No…
4. This is a strong argument from authority.

Example 2: Michael Jordan was on a commercial saying "Hanes underwear are the best." Therefore, I will love this new Hanes underwear I just bought.

Analysis:
1. Conclusion: I will love this new Hanes underwear.
2. The arguer cites a statement by Michael Jordan about Hanes underwear.

3. This is a very weak argument. Michael Jordan is not a knowledgeable source regarding the quality of underwear. Even if he wears and likes Hanes underwear, that is very weak support for the claim that I will like Hanes underwear.
4. This is a weak argument by authority, sometimes called "appeal to unqualified authority."

Egoist Fallacy

A) Form: The Egoist Fallacy is a version of an argument from authority. In this case, the person cited is *yourself*.
B) Fallacy: In some instances, you may be an authority on an issue. But most of the time, the egoist fallacy amounts to the argument "X is true because I believe it is true." This argument is very weak. Everyone believes many things to be true that are in fact false, so the fact that a person believes something is not in itself good evidence that what is believed is true.

Example: Person 1: I think gay marriage should be ratified in every state.
Person 2: Oh, why do you think that?
Person 1: Well, it just seems obvious to me that gay marriage should be allowed.

Analysis:
1. Conclusion: Gay marriage should be allowed (in every state).
2. The arguer supports his or her point by saying "it seems obvious to me...".
3. This argument is very weak. That doesn't mean that the conclusion is wrong or false, it just means that this person has provided very little evidence to support the conclusion. The fact that this person believes the conclusion does not provide evidence to support the conclusion being true.
4. This is an Egoist Fallacy.

Dichotomy (Disjunction) arguments

A) Form:
1. A dichotomy argument presents an either/or choice, one of which is usually an obviously bad choice, in order to get the listener to accept the other choice.
2. Dichotomy arguments are based on the deduction rule, disjunctive syllogism; A or B; Not A (or, "you don't want A");

therefore, B. Dichotomy arguments interesting arguments in that they are formally valid. The problem in bad dichotomy arguments is that the disjunction presented in the premises is not true – there are other options. So, technically, they are valid but unsound deductive arguments.

3. NOTE: Dichotomy arguments are often posed as conditionals; "If this doesn't happen, then this won't happen", or "If you want this, then do this".

B) Evaluation: Are the two choices presented really the only two choices? If the two choices presented are not the only two choices, the argument commits the fallacy of False Dichotomy. If the two choices presented are the only two choices, the argument is a strong Dichotomy argument.

Example 1: President Obama: "Either we invade Syria right now or terrorists will overrun the world."

Analysis:
1. Conclusion: We have to invade Syria right now.
2. The arguer supports his conclusion by saying the only other option is to allow terrorists to overrun the world.
3. Whether or not we invade Syria, terrorists are unlikely to overrun the world. The choices given are not the only possibilities.
4. This is a false dichotomy fallacy.

Example 2: Parent to child: "Either you turn down your music right now, or you'll be grounded."

Analysis:
1. The conclusion is "you should turn your music down."
2. The parent supports her/his conclusion by offering an unwanted alternative.
3. This is a good argument (assuming the parent will follow through). The dichotomy presented is a true dichotomy.
4. This is a strong dichotomy.

Causal arguments

A) Form:
1. Event B has followed event A in the past.
2. Event A has just happened.
3. Therefore, event B will happen.

B) Evaluation: Causal arguments are very tricky. Technically, the distinction is, if event A *causes* event B, then the argument is strong; if event B only follows event A by coincidence, then the argument is weak. But problems arise when we ask what it means to "cause" something. The philosopher David Hume famously pointed out that causation is really just a description of the way we experience things. If I put a tray of water in my freezer, it has been my experience that it will be ice when I get up the next morning. But can I be sure that will happen next time? Hume says "No." So he was very skeptical about causation. Another problem is, often we see strong correlations between events, but we can't be sure what the causal connection is. Then, how sure can we be that event B will follow event A in the future? Because of these difficulties, causal arguments are divided into three categories:

1. Strong causation. The connection between event A and event B is understood to be causal, so we have a strong reason to believe that event B will follow event A in the future.
2. Weak/no causation. The connection between event A and event B is understood NOT to be causal. We don't have strong reasons to believe that event B will follow event A in the future.
3. Partial causation. There seems to be some causal correlation between events, but we don't yet understand what the causal link is. The strength of the argument depends on the strength of the causal correlation.

Example 1: A significant number of children who play violent video games act out violently. Therefore, we should not allow children to play violent video games.

Analysis:
1. Conclusion: We should not allow children to play violent video games.
2. The arguer supports the conclusion by citing a correlation between playing violent video games and acting violently.
3. The strength of this argument is a matter of much debate. The correlation between playing violent video games and acting more violently is well established. But the causal connection is not clear. Maybe the children who act violently after playing violent video games would be violent anyway.
4. If the violent children would be violent anyway, the argument would be a weak false-cause or partial-cause argument. If playing the games makes children violent, then there would be a causal

correlation, and it would be strong. We don't really know right now.
So this is at best a weak causal argument at this point.

Example 2: The high school football team fans all wore pink ribbons
for the first three games of the season and the football team won.
That means that if the fans all wear pink ribbons the rest of the
season, we'll have a winning season.

Analysis:
1.   Conclusion: If the fans wear pink ribbons the team will win.
2.   The arguer supports her argument by citing the correlation between
     the first three games and the fans wearing pink ribbons.
3.   There is clearly a correlation between the ribbons and the winning.
     But is it a causal or a coincidental correlation? The fans wearing
     pink ribbons cannot *cause* the football team to play differently.[15]
     The correlation is coincidental.
4.   This is a false cause fallacy.

Generalization arguments

A) Form:
    1.   Group A has quality or characteristic X.
    2.   Therefore, Group B (a larger group that A is part of) also has
        quality or characteristic X.
B) Evaluation: To "generalize" means to move from smaller, or more
    specific, to larger, or more general. In a generalization argument, a
    quality or characteristic that applies to a small group is said to apply
    to a larger group as well. One of the most common places we see
    generalization arguments in our culture is opinion polls in the news.
    The argument there is, since X% of the people we polled say Y, X%
    of the city or state or nation think Y. Polls and generalizations are
    very difficult to validate and are usually fairly weak arguments. The
    two areas where they generally fail are:
    1.   The sample group is too small. If I want to know how many
        Californians favor gay marriage and I poll 3 people, I am not
        going to get a valid result, because 3 people is too few to
        accurately represent the whole state. How many are enough?

---

[15] It is possible that the pink ribbons are commemorating something, like the death of
a football player or coach, and that remembering that person is making the players
play better. But even then, the ribbons are not causing the play or the wins – they are
causing a memory, which is causing the difference in play.

This is a very difficult question. Generally, the more, the better. But for a large population like a city or state or country, a poll of a few thousand will give a margin of error of about 5% (the poll number is within 5% of the actual number) and it is very difficult to get the margin of error less than 5%.

2. The sample group is biased, or doesn't represent the large group accurately. If I want to know how many Californians favor gay marriage and I poll several thousand residents of San Francisco, my poll is not going to be accurate, because residents of San Francisco will have a tendency to favor one side of the issue over the other. On the other hand, if I poll several thousand residents of a very conservative suburb of Los Angeles, my poll is not going to be accurate, because residents of a conservative suburb of Los Angeles will have a tendency to favor one side of the issue. The rule is, EVERY member of the target group must have an equal chance of being selected for the poll, or it will be biased.

Example 1: I have met 3 people from Texas and they all had great senses of humor. I guess Texans in general have great senses of humor.

Analysis:
1. Conclusion: Texans have greats senses of humor.
2. The arguer supports his or her conclusion by citing 3 instances of Texans with great senses of humor.
3. This is a weak argument. The problem is, the sample group is too small. 3 people are not enough to support the generalization. This is how stereotypes are created. Someone noticed some quality that a few people from a certain group had, and generalized to all the members of that group. Stereotypes are always examples of weak generalizations.
4. This is a weak generalization fallacy.

Example 2: Fox News surveyed people who watch their program and 76% of them say that they don't favor increased taxes. Therefore, Americans don't want increased taxes.

Analysis:
1. Conclusion: Americans don't want increased taxes.
2. The arguer supports his or her conclusion by citing a poll of Fox News watchers.

3. This is a weak argument. We don't know how many people were polled, but the bigger problem here is that Fox News watchers are a biased group. That doesn't mean they're bad, just that they don't accurately represent ALL Americans. Similarly, if the New York Times polled its readership, the sample group would also be biased and the generalization would be weak.
4. This is a weak generalization fallacy.

Slippery Slope arguments

A) Form
1. Arguer argues that if we allow A to happen, then X, Y, and Z will happen.
2. Arguer claims that Z would be bad.
3. Arguer argues that since we don't want X, Y, and/or Z to happen, we shouldn't do/accept A.
4. Slippery Slopes, like Dichotomy arguments, are valid deductively. They It illustrates one of the rules of Natural Deduction. Consider this pattern: If A, then B. B is bad (or not-B), therefore, avoid A (not-A). Which rule is this?
5. Evaluation: As an example of a formal deduction rule, they are valid. That is, IF event A will lead to event Z, and Z is bad, then A is bad. So the problem is not with the inference. That means that the problem must be with the truth of the premises, making it unsound. Usually, it is unlikely (or at least no evidence has been provided) that X, Y, or Z will really happen, so they do not support the conclusion that we should not do A.
6. Slippery slope arguments have elements of both Straw Man (distorting the argument) and Red Herring (leading the argument away from the real issue) fallacies. But they are a more specific form, and should be identified as slippery slopes.

B) Non-fallacious slippery slope arguments
1. If it is likely (or evidence has been provided) that X, Y, and/or Z will actually happen, and if we don't want them to happen, then there is good support for rejecting A, and the argument is not fallacious.

Example: Never buy a lottery ticket. People who buy lottery tickets soon find that they want to gamble on horses. Next, they develop a strong urge to go to Las Vegas and bet their life savings in casinos. The addiction to gambling gradually ruins their family life. Eventually they die, homeless and lonely.

Analysis:
1. Conclusion: Never buy a lottery ticket.
2. The arguer tries to convince the listener of the conclusion by listing bad things that will result from buying a ticket.
3. This is a bad argument – the chain of events listed is very unlikely, so the conclusion is not supported.
4. This is a slippery slope fallacy.

Non-fallacious example:
If you contract the HIV virus, it will latch on to your immune cells and inject its genetic material into them. The HIV material will then take over the cell, disable it, and use it as a factory to produce copies of itself. These copies will, in turn, attack other immune cells and repeat the process. Eventually, your immune system will become so weakened that will easily contract other infections and diseases. The result will be that you will become very sick and likely die. Therefore, you should avoid contracting HIV.

Analysis:
1. Conclusion: You should avoid contracting HIV.
2. The arguer tries to convince the listener of the conclusion by listing bad things that will result from contracting HIV.
3. This is a good argument – the chain of events listed is well-supported scientifically and medically, so the conclusion is strongly supported.
4. This is a slippery slope argument, but not a fallacy.

Exercises

1. Bill says that if we support his investment program, our investment will pay great dividends. Then we will become rich and can quit our jobs and live on a luxury yacht for the rest of our lives. I think we should do it.
2. Bill says that we should invest in his investment program. He says that Bob Jones, the famous Rock musician, looked at it and fully endorses it.
3. Bill says that we should invest in his investment program. He says that Bob Jones, the well-known economist, looked at it and claims that it is very likely to be successful.
4. Why is gay marriage wrong? Because it makes me sick, that's why!
5. I spent a week traveling in Germany. All of the people in every restaurant I ate in were very friendly and welcoming. I think the Germans are a very friendly people.

6. If we raise taxes to decrease the budget deficit, then investors will have less money to invest in business. Then business will slow down, which means that people will make even less money, which will mean a worse economy AND less tax revenue. Raising taxes is a bad idea!

7. If we cut back on government spending to decrease the budget deficit, then we will have less money to spend on social programs for the poor, needy, and uneducated. That means that we will be harming the people that need us most, and a less educated workforce will mean a worse economy. We must continue to help the people that need us!

8. My brother said that there are three workers from Guatemala working on the construction crew that he is on. I guess the Guatemalans are taking over our construction industry.

9. I forgot to turn the headlights off on my car last night (and it doesn't turn them off by itself!). I expect the battery to be dead this morning.

10. Last May, a school of sardines got stranded in Long Beach harbor and all died. I guess we should expect this to happen every May now.